UNVEILED
A JOURNEY TO SOUL REALIZATION

UNVEILED

A JOURNEY TO SOUL REALIZATION

HERB COHEN

Unveiled: A Journey to Soul Realization

© 2025 by Herb Cohen

All rights reserved. No portion of this publication may be reproduced, stored in a retrieval system, or transmitted by any means—electronic, mechanical, photocopying, recording, or any other—except for brief quotations in printed reviews, without the prior written permission of the publisher.

Library of Congress Control Number: 2025908617
ISBN: 978-1-964686-53-0 (paperback) 978-1-964686-54-7 (ebook)

Although this publication is designed to provide accurate information about the subject matter, the publisher and the author assume no responsibility for any errors, inaccuracies, omissions, or inconsistencies herein. This publication is intended as a resource; however, it is not intended as a replacement for direct and personalized professional services.

Editors: Jennifer Casey, Stephanie Thompson
Cover and Interior Design: Emma Elzinga

The cover picture is a channeled painting by the author and emits a vortex of energy that can be experienced simply by holding the cover in front of you.

Printed in the United States of America

First Edition

3 West Garden Street, Ste. 718
Pensacola, FL 32502
www.indigoriverpublishing.com

Ordering Information:

Quantity sales: Special discounts are available on quantity purchases by corporations, associations, and others. For details, contact the publisher at the address above.

Orders by US trade bookstores and wholesalers: Please contact the publisher at the address above.

With Indigo River Publishing, you can always expect great books, strong voices, and meaningful messages. Most importantly, you'll always find . . . *words worth reading*.

CONTENTS

Introduction XI

PART I FOUNDATION XVII

   1 **Ego** 1

       The Dilemma of Being Separate 1
       Rancid Food 2
       Urgency and Personal Responsibility 8
       Consciousness Versus Mind 11
       Exploring Possibility 16
       Placebo and Healing 17
       Limiting Possibility 20
       The Ego Lens 22
       The Filter System 25

   2 **Awareness** 31

       The Awareness Lens 31
       Ego 34
       Awareness: 34
       Compassion 35
       Lessons 36
       Human Death, Soul Continuance 37
       Past Lives: Lessons via Soul Memory 40
       Ways We Can Learn Lessons 42
       Divinity Within Atrocity 45
       War 49
       Personal Atrocities 50
       Dissolution of Separateness 52

Part II Exercises ... 59

3 Coping and Healing ... 61

Working With Energy ... 61
Pause ... 62
Flow: Rapid Grounding ... 62
Flowing ... 63
Flow as a Healing Tool ... 65
Working With the Merkaba ... 66
Combining Flow with the Merkaba to Heal ... 68
Being In Flow ... 70
Working with God as a Spiritual Understanding ... 72

Part III Conscious Awareness ... 77

4 Preparing For Soul Lens ... 79

Introduction to Consciousness ... 79
Consciousness Beyond This Life ... 80
Surrendering to Get Out of the Way ... 81
Trust and Letting ... 84
Breathing Exercise ... 88
Knowing and Truth ... 89
Service ... 92
Frequency and Dimension ... 94

Part IV Preparing for Soul Connection ... 99

5 Soul Lens ... 101

Intro to Soul ... 102
Our Aura ... 104
Expanding Our Experience of Being ... 105
Intuition ... 107
Three Lenses ... 108
An Example of Three Lenses ... 109
Expansion and Contraction ... 110

An Extreme Example of Contraction and Expansion 113
Timelines 116
Contexts 119
Emptiness, Energy, Form. 122
An Experiential Exercise 123
Reality via Manifestation 124
Limitation 125
Conscious vs. Unconscious Manifestation 127
Love as Energy 130
Tonglen: Practicing Loving Compassion. 132
Being Love 134
Change 137
Play and Creativity 140
Freedom 142
Freedom as a Self-Identified Experience 143
Those Who Are Not Free 147
Finding Our Purpose 149
Divine Feminine, Divine Masculine 150
Deepening Surrender 151
Free Will Versus Divine Will 155
Arts, Music, Creativity 157
The Others 160

Part V Soul and Beyond 163

6 Soul Connection 165

Connection to Our Soul 165
Deepening Conscious Awareness. 167
Realizing Our Soul 169
Daily Practice: Connect With Your Soul 172
Released Soul Contracts 172
Soul Incarnations 176

7 Paradigm of Truth..................................181
    Truth as a Paradigm....................181
    Personal Truths............................182
    Collective Truths..........................182
    Universal Truths..........................183
    The Truths Continuum 184
    Valuation 184
    Sovereignty 186
    Surrender...................................188

Epilogue..191
Letter from the Author...........................195
Bibliography 197

Without darkness, we would have no idea what light is.

Dedicated to you, the reader.

INTRODUCTION

When I started my practice as a trauma therapist, guiding people as they healed from profound traumatic events had a powerful impact on me. The shift I experienced deepened a journey that began years earlier.

After graduating from art school, I had no vocational ideas or plans, so I took a summer job at a camp in New Hampshire. On his way to visit me, my cousin and childhood buddy suffered a fatal head-on collision. My first experience with trauma and significant loss left me shaken and experiencing intense pain. I did not understand why life decided to turn sharply in such a dark direction. I was confronted with a barrage of questions about death, and no answers. I eventually sought professional help.

Over almost forty years of working with mental health, addiction, and trauma, I have pondered similar questions from my clients. It seems common for people who grew up with traumatic events in childhood to repeatedly experience similar traumatic events as adults. As we attempt to process dark and uncomfortable aspects of their lives, they ask many *why* questions. *Why did all this bad stuff happen to me? Why am I so unlucky?*

I did not have the answers to these familiar questions, but I helped people accept they may never know the answers either. I helped them accept that whatever happened in the past is over. They can move on.

When I began as a therapist, I did not know I would take that question and turn it into the topic of a book. I did not know how much I would learn by witnessing my clients' healing and their ascension from trauma and addiction to higher states of consciousness. I did not know that I would discover that the worst traumas I would experience would be the traumas I lived through in past lives. I did not know deep and powerful meanings would be revealed through my practice, changing my life forever.

This book looks at the evolution and transformation of self through a spiritual journey of ascension and connection to your soul. It is written from a spiritual view. As a licensed professional, I cannot abandon science. However, this book is about surrendering to the spiritual, and "science" has been somewhat jettisoned in the writing process. I have been influenced by science and can see how all this pulls together. I am trained and very informed in how our brain works and intersects with ego activation, and how energy and emotion impact our nervous system. These are all considered in this text as science, though when I get into talking about soul and consciousness, I move away from evidenced-based knowledge by necessity. I am hopeful that one day soon, what is scientific will be able to merge with what is spiritual. As a note of caution, there may be parts that seem controversial or traumatic in nature, for some the material may even seem offensive, though I hope that is not the case. I just want to be clear that there are some extraordinary stories and points of view presented.

This book is something we *do*—we practice as opposed to just read. It provides both a path and a map for you to find meaning and purpose in your life, regardless of your lived experience. Practicing faithfully will bring you to a higher state of consciousness and connect you with your soul. You will learn to communicate with your soul and be able to spend the rest of your life deepening this relationship. To aid the learning process, I created a few new terms.

The information presented in this book is intuitively sourced. It represents *my* view, and it comes from my heart. Therefore, the best way to access this material is to bring the information into your heart to be realized as knowing. If you read the material and intellectually attempt to make sense of it, you are more likely to not integrate it.

Ideas and beliefs regarding what is possible will be questioned and challenged. You may find some of this information challenging or difficult, but I encourage you to keep an open mind. This is my truth. In Paul Selig's books, his guides conveyed this idea that what is true is always true, always will be true, and cannot be untrue. Truth can be described as controversial but cannot be anything but true.

As the therapeutic process nears its end, my clients often look back and reflect on their incredible journey.

Here is a share from a former client:

"As I sipped a glass of wine, its smell alone was a welcome relief. I could feel the wine's effect, the intoxicating feeling from the top of my head to and throughout my body as I took another drink. I felt a warmth that I imagined a child felt when she snuggled up safely in her mom's lap. I never felt that, so the warmth alcohol brought was welcomed, and its numbing ability allowed me to stop remembering that I did not know what a mother's warmth felt like. I looked forward to not feeling, not remembering, not being in so much horrific pain.

"When I finally tired of suffering and realized the numbing alcohol provided was not helping me move forward in my life, I decided to act. I went to AA meetings and put drinking aside, but then had to feel the result of a painful set of life experiences growing up. The painful experiences were in the past—I knew that—yet they hurt as though all of it was happening now. I was angry that my life hurt so much, and at times took that out on others and attracted relationships triggering part of me I did not want to feel or experience. Why was this happening to me? I was a good little girl, who only sought to be loved, protected, and respected. Why was that so difficult? Why did I live under such darkness, and why did it follow me wherever I went? I decided to find a therapist that could help me stop suffering. Talk [therapy] did not seem to help, so I did some research, and that is how I met Herb.

"He seemed very confident my struggles would resolve, though I felt exceptionally broken and beyond repair. He provided some education about trauma, addiction, neurobiology, and energy. Then I learned coping skills that provided immediate, though temporary, relief. We went through stages of preparation to go into deeper therapeutic processes that would include EMDR, Brainspotting, and Hypnotherapy. I was amazed at how my mind stepped in to change memories to have more favorable outcomes. I was confronting my past head-on, weekly, and can say it was hard work. It was painful at times, but the repair, the new ideas of who I was, always felt good. It took a while, but I could feel a shift happening as I reinvented who I was. I struggled—and still do—with AA meetings defining me as an alcoholic without addressing underlying traumas. Alcohol was not to be blamed; it was not about drugs or alcohol. I could not say anything, though I could feel myself moving beyond such simple definition.

"I was introduced to that warm feeling, only not from a mother or a drink. It came from within. I learned, or 'remembered' as Herb would say, that I *am* love.

"As we neared the end of that treatment period, I could reflect on all the remarkable times in my life, all the negative events as well as the positives. I could see they all had a purpose. Even drinking was perfectly what I needed at that time. I realized I would not be the person I am now if not for all that happened. I could see that this was not haphazard, but deliberate, and the meaning emerged from what I learned by processing those events. This evolutionary process is continuing, and I am learning and growing. My new lessons are not as harsh; I am not afraid to engage them. I now know there is something worthy about embracing whatever resistance comes my way.

"I left therapy, and my energy level was higher. I did not feel pain anymore. I could allow myself to feel spiritual and good. This shift in energy had a direct impact on my family. My son watched as

I transformed from an angry, fear-based mom to a loving, unconditionally supportive, and protective mother he needed me to be. He has changed, and I see the direct impact my transformation has had on him. My husband was also living with an equally disturbing past, and, oddly, he became worse. My higher energy seemed to trigger his descent, and he became rageful and hurtful. He escalated and was ultimately given an ultimatum to seek help. Herb explained his soul prompted this acting out to force him to be responsible so it too could evolve. I was watching it happen before my eyes, and now he is engaged in healing and evolving.

"I can see how my changes and shifts in energy have directly impacted and changed people around me, as well as the choices and decisions I make. I am empowered in knowing I can choose what I want to experience. I can see my reality has shifted. Herb's book explains how what happened to me is meaningful. He takes us on a journey outside of actual processing and releasing to changing views, or 'lenses' as he phrases it. The insights are deep, and I can say after reading it, I am not ready to get all of it yet. This book moves from trauma to beyond recovery. It embraces a spiritual view of both, us, and the world we live in. This book bravely takes on the task of understanding the meaning of suffering, regardless of what suffering is to you. It may be at the level of atrocity or simply disappointment. If we can understand atrocity, we can understand lesser challenges.

"Herb draws from all his experience, both professionally and personally, and holds nothing back as he rolls ideas that reframe what we thought we knew to be seen differently. As you read further, he pulls you in deeper and deeper. This is not light reading but essential. We are becoming aware of our suffering, and now we are being presented with a map to not only heal but to evolve and grow spiritually. I advise as you read, go slow, and allow yourself to absorb the lessons before moving forward. This book is a deep journey into discovering who you truly are. I hope you discover new and beautiful versions of yourself, as I have."

—C.A., 2020

PART 1

FOUNDATION

Chapter 1

EGO

THE DILEMMA OF BEING SEPARATE

The polarization we experience in our society and in politics has grown more intense and does not feel good. If we dive into the chemistry of such, we see there is a flavor that colors the separateness. Fear-based thinking underlies and drives intolerance, resulting in polarization and separateness. This is parallel to how ego functions, as this component of our mind acts in a protective manner. One role of ego is to keep us safe.

There have been many times when our country was polarized: during the Vietnam War and before and after the Civil War are two dramatic examples. What is different today is having 24-hour access to news and social media. The internet and media act as amplifiers, making stories seem more extreme by stroking fear. Fear sells, so getting the public's attention using fear has become a deliberate function of media.

On a personal level, let's say I have an idea, and you have a different belief—no big deal. If you view my idea as threatening, then you would act in a protective manner and perhaps counterattack with your own different view. If we multiply this to a group, we now have polarized groups as people with similar ideas are packing together. We pack together because, like herd animals, the pack offers protection. On a global level, wars are one herd threatened by another. Unlike animals that herd to protect against another species of predator, we must herd to protect against other humans. We see herding behavior in political parties in government. We see society separating into sub-herds, amplifying a sense of separateness.

Ego is the I(me) experience of being. Ego identifies through our past and experiences itself as unique and separate. Ego will use the past to trigger a need to protect, as ego has a primary role as a protector.

Now let's backtrack to society in relation to this I(me) concept. We can now frame society as a collective of egos who have chosen to be separate from each other because they each feel a threat to who they are and how they self-identify. If we look at what each group is reacting to, we see fear-based thinking because our ego says I am separate from you, and you are separate from me. Our ego scans for threats and the need to herd, attack, or run away.

News flash! Ego is simply an *idea* and does not actually exist as a three-dimensional form. I will provide evidence of that later in the book. If ego does not actually exist, then I am not separate from you or anyone else, regardless of our different ideas. Understanding this would cause a huge shift, as I would no longer be threatened by your different ideas or beliefs. We could still disagree—and that would be okay—but the intolerance would disappear. If our government grasped this, it could pass bills, and be productive. There could be dialogue and healthy debate about differences. A nice daydream, I know, but let's look deeper into how ego can distort and obstruct our path.

Rancid Food

I witnessed a relationship where one partner was hostile and abusive, yet my client had not been successful in leaving him. She struggled to understand why this was so difficult for her, and I suggested a deeper look into why she found herself attracted to someone who treated her with so much disrespect.

Because ego is a protector, it makes an executive decision to avoid the pain of being alone, being unattended to, over being hurt within the relationship. Ego's judgment is often selective and reactive. It bases its decisions on past distortions rather than viewing the present reality. The result is confusing because my client knows this relationship is bad, but the "I" makes her believe she should stay. She fears being alone will be worse. She has stumbled upon a life lesson that will soon have deeper meaning. The lessons—"I don't deserve to be treated with respect" and "I am not good enough"—have roots in her past, and now she exposes an opportunity to realize that these negative ideas are untrue. Let us explore what happens in our brain, how we can learn from these experiences, and how these experiences can be as toxic as eating rancid food.

When we eat rancid or rotten food, it may look fine on the outside, but we face a harsh and disgusting reality when we take the first bite. We immediately notice our mouth lighting up with flavors and sensations, screaming to us that what we have eaten should not be consumed. It tastes so strong we may have to rinse our mouth or eat something else to purge the flavor. This informs us to cast this food aside or we will get sick. It is a form of suffering, only here, suffering serves a positive purpose. When we are triggered and experience emotional pain, something similar happens. The suffering lets us know there's something we need to pay attention to and possibly avoid. It is equivalent to the rancid taste in food. It lets us know that if we continue to engage, we will get sick, just as if we eat food that is rancid. The suffering protects us just as the rancid taste protects us. In the example above, the client experiences this when her boyfriend is mean and hurtful. Her kneejerk reaction is to run away and to leave him.

We learn from our experience; exposure to a toxic person does not feel good and can even trigger us to feel even worse. The lesson in tasting rotten food is that I must throw it away lest I get sick. The lesson here is similar. "If I stay in this relationship, I will continue to feel bad and even eventually develop sickness as a result." Yet many I work with continue to stay engaged in such relationships. They feel stuck, so they do not act on the lesson before them.

What is happening in our brain that keeps us stuck?

If we grow up with caregivers who are emotionally absent, neglectful, or toxic and abusive, or if we are repeatedly exposed to dangerous or humiliating experiences, our brains change to protect us. Our brain has two identical sides but assigns different functions to the right and left. Survival and emotional regulation work mostly through the right side. So, the right emotional alarm (a*mygdala*) increases in size to create more vigilance so we stay hyper-aware of possible danger, invalidation, dismissal, and so on. Next to amygdala sits the *hippocampus*, our memory distributor, which is covered in cortisol receptors. Cortisol and adrenaline are chemicals released in the brain on orders by amygdala to tell us we are in danger and to act. This is experienced as anxiety and/or anger, and if we feel overwhelmed with it, we may become depressed or numb. This is the rancid taste! The hippocampus absorbs these chemicals so we can feel normal again. But with repeated trauma, those chemical receptors fold in and lose the ability to switch off distress. The rancid taste does not disappear. You notice when someone feels triggered and they have a difficult time calming down.

With repeated exposure to distress, our brain activates more protection: the implicit memory system. We all have an implicit memory system. This is where we take a picture of each of the offensive events and store it in a region of the brain behind our right ear. Along with pictures are videos, sounds, physical sensations, emotions, and ideas about how we thought about ourselves at that moment. All are stored in this region on shelves filed by the associations of how we self-regarded at that moment. All the *I'm not good enough* memories are on one shelf, *I am not loveable* sits on another, and so on. These implicit memories have a special status. The amygdala protects them from being changed or deleted. They act as filters or triggers for future offenses to trigger a reaction and alarm us we are endangered again. Cortisol releases, and we are emotionally activated. When triggered, our alarm tells us we just took a bite of something rancid. It is no different from eating something rotten, except, with food, we instinctively throw it away rather than keep eating.

Why do we not run away from our abuse or neglect instinctively?

When the alterations in our brain take place, they interrupt our learning with distortions held by implicit memory. If I grow up neglected or abused by my caregivers, I learn I am not worthy of such love, so when I attract someone to be in a relationship with, I find someone abusive. I do not know what love is and may feel uncomfortable with it. This abuse is familiar to me, so I feel safe even though it does not feel good. The implicitly held distortions override our instinct to run away. As a child, I could not run away—where would I live? Running away was more dangerous than staying, so that is what we learn. The memories act as filters, screening my current experience, and setting off the alarm if something similar occurs. The new experience of rancid may be sourced in our past, as in this example.

Using this as a metaphor for being triggered now suggests that there is another lesson being presented when we taste rancidity. However, in this case, we don't leave, thus we are not learning the lesson before us. If we understand that the rancid taste of bad food protects us from getting sick, perhaps we can bridge this idea to emotional pain as having a protective function.

Within my journey of past life experiences, alongside integrated teachings of mentors and books, I developed ideas about our soul's journey from the afterlife in taking up a human form. These teachings are important, as they recognize what happened to us as something deliberate and purposeful.

When our soul takes on a human life (incarnation), it agrees to a contract of lessons it seeks to accomplish via the incarnation. Such as… "Am I loveable? Do I deserve to have fun and abundance?" They may be about moving past challenges we were born into or limitations we need to overcome. If I experience a toxic situation in which I feel unworthy, it feels bad because it is not true. If we dive into our story, we will discover the source of this and learn *I was a little kid who was not given the love and validation I should have received*. I did nothing to be unworthy, did not act unworthy, yet my young mind assumed this must be true, as another option might be that my parents don't love me. That feels far worse, so we go for blaming ourselves and end up learning a false idea of being unworthy. Rancid experiences point to what we need to learn to evolve as souls.

What if I distract myself from this rancid taste or numb it with drugs and/or alcohol?

I may have learned how to dissociate or numb at will. If I stuff away this emotion and deny anything is wrong, I can develop a physical illness or depression. If I do not taste the emotion, I will not know it is rotten. I will not learn my lesson and will continue to have rancid experiences. The client above decided not to leave her boyfriend, despite knowing he will be hurtful again. What if I know the abusive person empowers themselves by being mean and abusive toward me and this is not about me? I then limit how much they affect me. I choose to not let this person take my power away. Now I do not eat the rancid food. I will not get sick. I realize a lesson before me—to lose this relationship. I can look deeper and see if there is an earlier lesson triggering my present reaction. Suffering can be our greatest teacher when we are ready to be the student.

I have learned that what is true about who we are usually feels good, and what is untrue does not. We see that toxic emotions are there to point out what is unhealthy and perhaps unsafe. They point to lessons we need to learn to evolve as a person and as a soul.

Becoming aware of what tastes rancid is step one, recognizing this moment has an ingredient that is not tasting good. I need to identify what that is and check in. Step two is asking, "Is this feeling true, or is this a re-experience of an earlier time in my life (a trigger)?" These filters or triggers are implicit memories and intend to be present for life. Step three is getting help. Talk therapy may be defeated by amygdala guarding these memories. Fortunately, there are memory-based therapies that can put amygdala to sleep so these memories can be changed and removed from implicit storage as triggers permanently. Examples of such are Hypnotherapy, EMDR Psychotherapy (Eye Movement, Desensitization and Reprocessing—a memory-based psychotherapy), Brainspotting, Sensorimotor Psychotherapy, and Somatic Experiencing to name a few. Seeing our life from a lesson-oriented perspective gives meaning to what happened to us. These therapies allow us to expose and change and release all the implicit memories holding distorted ideas of who we are. We can see that these were experiences we needed to have to realize who we are.

There are other examples of rancidity we may experience besides emotional distress. It may be too dangerous as young children to protest what happens or cry or express how we feel at that moment. The mind recognizes the danger and asks our body to help. Thus, implicit memories can be stored in the body. I have seen people with inflamed colons, Crohn's Disease, and thyroid and adrenal disorders. Each organ and disease had three hours of related trauma memories, which were stored implicitly within. The memories documented why these organs or diseases acted to shut down or protect the individual at that time. Diseases often have a source in emotionally painful events. Unfortunately, most doctors prioritize treating physical symptoms and do not look beyond them to causal ideas.

In a society where collectives feel threatened by other ideas, we can see that they may be reacting to some past threat being triggered. Thus, there is a strong emotional charge. We are witnessing collective groups seeking safety in numbers.

It is our responsibility to do this work and self-realize. It is our responsibility to be the best version of ourselves to make this a better world.

Urgency and Personal Responsibility

One aspect of our personal responsibility is knowing that when we tap into our greater capacity to change, we impact others. Haven't you known someone who sobered up or began a combination of eating well and exercising, and, as a result, looks and feels amazing? We may inspire others, who were not even considering doing so, to change. When we are around people who inspire us, we feel energized, and we expand. In contrast, when we are around someone who is down and focused on negativity, we feel drained and depleted. They zap whatever positive energy we have. Imagine living in a world of beings who make us feel good. Imagine going to work and not seeing anyone who judges you or treats you as less than. Imagine a boss who cheers you on, supports your ideas, and encourages you to actualize them. You would feel excited, and, in turn, that would have a chain reaction to those around you.

Motivation to change has two key ingredients: urgency and hope. We may be suffering and have significant urgency to change our experience. In contrast, we may be financially secure and comfortable but hope for a sense of bliss within our capacity. If we want to change our lifestyle, eat healthier, and add exercise to our routine, we may have trouble making that adjustment sustainable, even though we know we will feel better. What is it that will shake us up to do things differently? On one end is a vision of what is possible—the idealized state (hope)—but that alone is not enough to move us to take that icebreaking first step. We need that sense of urgency that warns us of being stuck, resuming suffering, or denying us the opportunity to rise above where we are at. We need to encourage the sense of "I have no choice but to change now." We need to hold that urgency up, see it clearly, and realize we are here temporarily. We have only a finite time within this human incarnation, and every moment not spent experiencing our greatest capacity of being is wasted suffering—hence, urgency. We can adjust by adding more urgency or hope as needed. We need to honor that this is a choice. Our choice is our individual responsibility—however, how many have been inspired by the actions of radical change taken by others?

How did we get here?

In my psychotherapy practice, I have seen a pattern. People suffer because their parents learned a maladaptive parenting style from their parents, who learned it from their parents, and so forth. They come to me to break the multigenerational pattern. They want to be better parents to their own children, knowing how they were raised did not feel good.

Are you part of such a chain of mis-attachments? You may never be aware of how you changed others' lives just by something you did, said, or by a minor gesture. Throughout our lifetime, we may impact hundreds of lives and never realize it. If we look at adults repeating what they experienced as children with their children, we see a clear example. It may have begun with their grandparents, or perhaps their great-grandparents, who their children never even met. Thus, the actions impact generations of families throughout many lifetimes. Generational influences can be negative, positive, or both.

Personal responsibility becomes a collective impact if we each take charge of what we need to learn. We need to understand that the challenges we are born into are not arbitrary, nor are they there to punish. They help us resolve something of utmost importance. We may ultimately learn how to realize our souls through these lessons.

Remember, challenges are like rancid food. The rancidness serves not to harm or punish but to lovingly protect.

Personal responsibility becomes a collective idea in the context of family, employment, school, or other social settings—including social media (internet). Who we are, how we act, affects others. If we join collective groups, we see influence of global significance. A personal story in the news can become the subject of multiple collective groups and go viral, gaining a global audience. Such can impact change worldwide. I'm suggesting we as a collective manifest global change by starting at the individual level. If many do this, we will have a collective influence and hopefully a global shift.

Personal responsibility includes being nice to those around me and not hurting anyone. Doctors take an oath to do no harm. Politicians should take such an oath, and perhaps we can add to that list and include drug manufacturers and insurance companies.

On October 4, 2023, ProPublica[1] reporter Anne Maria Barry-Jester broke a story that speaks to the responsibility of "do no harm" we assume to be inherent in pharmaceutical companies. In 2018, researcher and scientist Dr. Neil Martinson took his tuberculosis vaccine to be developed and distributed by pharmaceutical manufacturer giant, Glaxo Smith Kline, Plc (GSK). GSK also had two other vaccines to develop—malaria and shingles—all sharing a key ingredient. The one problem: This ingredient was in limited supply, so a decision had to be made. Tuberculosis and malaria would have a market that would be poor and mostly target African nations who were unable to pay higher premiums than shingles could yield in an American market. As a result, the shingles vaccine became a multi-billion dollar hit for GSK, which did not permit access to others to develop vaccines for tuberculosis and malaria. It is estimated that one million children will be lost in Africa each year because of diseases such as malaria and tuberculosis. The CDC says less than one hundred people will die of shingles this year. We see that GSK honored its responsibility to its shareholders rather than prioritizing human lives. Money is more valuable than human life in the world of pharmaceutical manufacturing. Imagine how much

---

1   Anne M. Barry-Jester, "How A Big Pharma Company Stalled a Potentially Life Saving Vaccine in Pursuit of Bigger Profits," ProPublica, October 4, 2023. https://www.propublica.org/article/how-big-pharma-company-stalled-tuberculosis-vaccine-to-pursue-bigge-profits.

money would be lost if cancer were curable. If I developed cancer, my options would be defined by a science that has already decided money is more important than my life.

Each of us should own and practice this idea of "doing no harm." It is our inherent responsibility. We have evolved God-like abilities to create as well as to destroy. A shift in our energy is a shift in the collective energy. This imparts us with a huge and urgent responsibility. Somehow, we seem to have forgotten this, or it has not been much of a priority. In engaging in separateness, we forget about others. We focus on ourselves, and our concept of responsibility shifts to support this. Later in this book, we will discuss being in the awareness part of our brain and see that the idea of being separate is just that—an idea. It leads us to the dilemmas we struggle with now as a collective, as a planet. When we see our role in the context of an Earth in trouble, we experience an urgency—an urgency for the planet and for the collective of Earth's inhabitants to shift *now*. Let us take a deeper look at our experience of being so we can explore new possibilities.

Consciousness Versus Mind

This book will engage exercises and address concepts involving consciousness and the mind.

To minimize confusion, I will provide definitions for labels that I will use. As a disclaimer, I am not creating new definitions, rather I will explain how I will refer to words meaningful to my approach to teach and advance ideas with greater clarity.

As I see it, the mind has three basic functions: *thinking* (frontal cortex), *feeling* (limbic), and *awareness* (outer cortex, parietal lobe). Thinking is necessary for the experience of ego (the I(Me) part). Our emotions enrich our experience of being an I, so ego works collaboratively with our thoughts, emotions, and historic memory. Awareness is our sensory experience of "being," using our sense organs in the outer cortexes of our brain. Conscious awareness is the awareness of being aware, and that is both within and outside of our brain. Let's say I smell a candle in an office down the hall. I am using awareness (my sense of smell) to notice. The candle smells like an apple pie baking (awareness). Now a memory presents of my mom baking apple pie, and I step into that memory, as it is pleasurable. I am now in my mind (limbic brain—old memory and emotional experience = ego). If I pause and reflect on what I am doing—how I am distracted by the scent into a past memory—I am being aware of being aware. The bigger picture of the whole scene is conscious awareness.

Theories regarding consciousness and the brain fall into two types. *Physicalist* theories are materialistic, observable, and empirical models. The brain is the source of creating and experiencing consciousness. I have seen scans of the "God spot" and know from the physicalists' research that consciousness can be measured with brain activation. We require the brain to experience consciousness and report those experiences. *Non-local* theories are currently emerging and have a premise that consciousness is not of brain origin but does not deny the brain as a source of experiencing this entity. The theories attached to these ideas looking at consciousness vary, but our purpose in studying this is to be open to evolving spiritually. I am not proposing a theory or philosophy that cannot be challenged. I am not writing to prove anything—only to reframe ideas and language we are used to so that we can be open to new possibilities of experience that support psychospiritual development.

I most align with the most recent research that has consciousness as existing independent of our brain.

Let us look at some recent theories that suggest consciousness is not local to our brain and some experiences that support that our brain is the key.

I do a therapy developed by Dr. David Grand called Brainspotting. If someone presents with an emotion, like anxiety, but they are not sure why, I ask them to drop into their body, notice where they feel this fear the strongest, and point to that spot. I take a long pointer with a bright-colored tip and ask them to follow the tip with their eyes only, keeping their head still. I move it at eye level, very slowly and in an arc, side-to-side, asking them to simultaneously notice the spot and to call out when the feeling jumps or intensifies. I stop at that point, and we refine where the pointer tip makes that spot on the body react strongest. I move the tip higher, lower, bring it further away, and close in until we locate the exact spot that is most activating. I turn on bilateral stimulation (in this case, I used hand buzzers) used for EMDR Psychotherapy, and they start releasing memory. This identifies the reason for feeling anxious. The spot we identified in space directly relates to a spot on their body and connects to a source memory in their brain. The spot disappears when we have finished processing. Though, sometimes the spot moves, and we follow it across the room until it no longer activates. I can find spots associated with positive emotions and sometimes use two spots at once.

If you look around you, noticing the space in the room, consider there may be spots presently associated with you. This challenges our ideas about mind, brain, and physical experiences. It brings into awareness the idea that an energetic field may connect us to what we interact with, regardless of if we are aware of it or not. We do not simply end where our skin ends. Only recently have physicists and scientists begun to employ quantum physics to explore this idea of a field through which information can be held and transmitted. Lynne McTaggart is a researcher whose books chronicle the historic leaps being made. Quantum physics employs subatomic particles and looks at information as energy in the form of particles and waves. These theories can greatly impact us on a human level, but for now, let's get back to consciousness theory.

Clifford Lazarus, PhD, cites the work of Dr. Peter Fenwick, a neuropsychiatrist who studied near-death experience (NDE) for fifty years as a medical doctor in a trauma unit. "Fenwick's view is that the brain does not create or produce consciousness but rather filters it. As odd as this idea might seem at first, there are some analogies that bring the concept into sharper focus. For example, the eye filters a very small sliver of the electromagnetic spectrum, and the ear registers only a narrow range of sonic frequencies. The brain filters and perceives only a tiny part of the Cosmo's intrinsic consciousness."[2]

That makes consciousness separate from the mind and brain. There are a lot of people studying NDE and accruing data common to death experiences reported by people who died and were resuscitated. A specialist in cardiac resuscitation, Dr. Sam Parnia, with NYU Langone Medical Center, has led investigations in people he has resuscitated. He noticed in his studies, under the AWAREness during REsussitation AWARE-II study, that people reported being lucid and had recall of separating from their body during NDEs.[3]

Dr. Eben Alexander, a neurosurgeon, noted that examining the CT scans and MRIs of his brain follow *his* NDE. "The level of destruction of my neocortex, the part according to conventional neuroscience, is most involved in our detailed human conscious experience of the world that would not permit any dream, hallucination, or drug effect."[4] In his book, *Proof of Heaven*, he describes a vivid journey as "super real," and this is a common feature in NDE reporting. Dr. Alexander is of the school of thought that consciousness is responsible for the universe; the physical world exists within consciousness. He agrees the brain acts as a filter, but at death, such a filter is no longer necessary nor available. After death, we learn that the consciousness we then experience is that of our soul. Our souls are eternal, so this makes perfect sense, though science has not caught up with finding

---

2   Clifford N. Larzarus, "Can Consciousness Exist Outside of the Brain?" Psychology Today. June 26, 2019. https://www.psychologytoday.com/us/blog/think-well/201906/can-consciousness-exist-outside-the-brain.

3   Greg Williams, "Patients Recall Death Experiences After Cardiac Arrest," NYU Langone Health, September 14, 2023. https://nyulangone.org/news/patients-recall-death-experience-after-cardiac-arrest.

4   Alexander E. III. Consciousness and the Shifting Scientific Paradigm. Paradigm Explorer Journal of the Scientific and Medical Network. 127; 2018, pp. 3–8.

evidence for a soul. "Questions concerning the soul, afterlife, reincarnation, God, and Heaven proved to be too difficult to answer through conventional scientific means, which implied that they might not exist. Likewise extended consciousness, remote viewing, extraordinary perception, psychokinesis, clairvoyance, telepathy, and pre-cognition have seemed stubbornly resistant to comprehend through 'standard' scientific investigation."[5]

Dr. Joe Dispenza documented in his books how structural, neurochemical, and energetic changes in our brain can enable profound visual and spiritual experiences. You and I right now are experiencing one energetic dimension—3D—though many levels of energetic experience can be achieved if we manifest vibrating at those frequencies. If we do some energy work and change the frequency running through us, we can experience another dimension simultaneously. It feels different.

I have gotten very good at living at a higher frequency and can now easily receive information from higher dimensions. This information clearly predates my tapping in, as it is timeless and exists independent of my access. No translation to linear time exists there, as time in that dimension is not linear. The information and the experience of it are both ancient and current at once. Our brains would struggle with this, and it is not sourced by my brain but may be received by it. I access this profound experience because I raised my frequency and used the energy field of my soul to move to a different dimension. I experience it with my entire body, including my brain. I have experienced a vastness so great it could not fit in our mind or brain. The limitlessness in higher consciousness takes us to experience everything beyond definition. Our inherent souls are free of the limitations we struggle with. This experience of consciousness is independent, but not separate. It is not separate because, as you will learn in this text, separateness does not exist. Our soul is not separate nor is what we experience via our soul.

---

5   Eben Alexander, Proof of Heaven (New York: Simon and Shuster, 2012), pp. 152–153.

Simply put, consciousness is the ground from which all exists. When we understand this, we are using conscious awareness. Understanding the difference between mind, brain, and consciousness lets us learn and overcome the limitations that hinder our brain's ability to filter and move beyond what we know is possible.

Exploring Possibility

What is possible is defined by what is not possible, just as light is defined by darkness. Whether automatically or unconsciously, we connect what is *not* possible to give it definition and justification. For example, I experienced I was running late after delay by a very long phone call, yet the clock registered I had not lost any time and was on time. My first thought was that the clock must have stopped, not that reality was bending.

Possibility often depends on who perceives the situation. At the extreme end, possibility questions what is real, especially if potential outcomes seem miraculous or beyond our definition of reality. Our beliefs are challenged when experience defies our perception of what is possible. Inevitably, such a moment will cause us to pause and, in confusion, question what we have witnessed.

After practicing a Qigong breathing exercise for a few hours while driving to a conference at a hotel near the Hudson River, one such moment occurred for me. I arrived early and was walking along the rocks at the river's edge when suddenly a screen came down over my mind's eye and showed the scene ahead of me. There was a body lying on the rocks! The screen quickly lifted, and then I walked further, and sure enough, a bloated body lay there, washed up upon the rocks. It turned out to be a dead dog. This happened again moments later, again sampling life before I experienced it. Then I experienced exactly what I previewed. That challenged my fixed, ironclad idea about time being linear. How could I experience a moment before I lived it? Does this mean linear time is an illusion? Do I know on some level what will happen next month, or next year? Perhaps it has already happened? Perhaps I have already written these words, and you have already read them. This micro experience rocked my understanding of being in the world as I knew it because I experienced what I thought was not possible. When we finally have such a moment, we are more open to what else is possible.

Placebo and Healing

Experiences we believed to be impossible now occur before our eyes, and we as a community, especially as a science-minded community, choose to not see them. In FDA studies submitted for approval, it is required that a control group with a placebo be included. In a placebo event, subjects (thousands at a time for each study) receive either medication or a dummy. Neither the subject nor the people giving the pills know which is which—thus, we consider it double-blind. Thirty percent of the time (placebo) people taking the dummy will believe they have taken the real medication—and this miraculously heals what needed correction. It matters not if the disease is cancer or something benign. This presentation of placebos demonstrates how the impossible happens with *a shift in belief and thus aligns their brain and body to heal.*

I have listened to so many pharmacy representatives present studies of their pharmaceuticals versus placebo. I was so blown away by the fact that a solid third of each study remitted all their symptoms of disease with a sugar pill, believing it was medication. The medication provided temporary relief while at the same time manifesting other disease states such as heart and metabolic disease. The placebo effect demonstrated that we could heal ourselves, and presentation after presentation, no matter what drug was tested, the placebo effect stayed at a solid 30 percent.

Our country spends billions of dollars researching more costly disease-causing chemicals yet spends comparatively nothing on researching the harmless cost-effective placebo effect so we can have safer, more affordable healthcare. Placebo shows we can remit almost any disease without chemicals, and it can be seen in every FDA-approved pharmaceutical's qualifying study. There are over one trillion documented placebo events. It is real, yet not well-researched or considered in terms of its greater implications (i.e., cancer). We urgently need to venture toward these possibilities.

Placebo is 30 percent of any group. The FDA has not demanded that researchers examine the possible placebo effect *within* the groups receiving experimental medication, which could show results of 30 percent placebo-induced improvement. The FDA grants approval if a drug or procedure can beat the placebo effect by 50 percent. Thus, if 30 percent remit symptoms on a sugar pill and 60 percent remit symptoms on medication, the medication will qualify for FDA approval. But if we viewed the medication group as a subgroup, then another 30 percent would possibly be placebo. The FDA does not require such discernment to take place. However, I popped this question to a pharmacy representative regarding a presentation on antidepressants. The Pharmacy representative said they follow FDA guidelines and sidestepped the reality I was presenting.

Let us take a study where 100 people with depression are studied, and half are given a medication, and the other half are given a sugar pill (placebo). Sixty percent of the subjects remit their depression on the medication (twice that of the 30 percent who took sugar pills). The medication becomes eligible for FDA approval. But within the 60 percent, it is possible that as a subgroup of medication takers, a placebo effect takes effect because the subjects believe the pill is helping them, whether it is or not. That would mean possibly 30 percent of the 60 percent who remitted depression did so, not because they took medication but because of placebo effect. If investigated and proven, the medication tested would fail FDA approval, as it is now, because, hypothetically, it is only 30 percent effective.

Ten years after I reflected on this, such inquiries came to pass. Meta studies flooded research journals after outpatient recipients of antidepressants (SSRIs) were asked if they still felt depressed. Thirty percent (which is placebo!) reported no longer being depressed while on the medication. This validates my theory that the experimental medication group is a subgroup within which a placebo effect takes place.

The FDA has not changed its methods or indications it has approved of such medications, despite an avalanche of research that challenges such studies submitted for approval. How many other FDA-approved medications have not considered the placebo effect within their medicated control groups? What about COVID-19 vaccination drug trials? They, too, needed to beat placebo by 50 percent. I am not anti-medication or anti-vax, and I am not a scientist, but my curious mind asks these simple questions that the experts at the FDA should be asking. They are charged with making sure these medications are safe and as efficacious as the manufacturers indicate.

This relates to the concept of what is possible as studies document placebo effects for drugs and procedures across the spectrum. It is amazing that we can have these results in studies regarding placebo and have none of it considered newsworthy. If we can control the placebo effect, we can heal or have people heal themselves, at little or no cost. Nine thousand people developed antibodies to COVID-19 on a pneumonia vaccine (used as placebo in the Pfizer trials). Isn't that, by itself, newsworthy? The shareholders of the pharmaceutical industry will not be too happy, as they have kept this information secret. Africa did not get any Pfizer vaccine, nor placebo, during the height of the pandemic when vaccines were being distributed. According to the World Health Organization, one-third of the world does not have access to medications due to pharmaceutical companies' greed.

We know the magic science can achieve; we know what *is* possible. Let us look at these placebo events that open limitless possibilities in healing. We can deliberately employ the components and receive a positive outcome 100 percent of the time. If I commit to the desired outcome as if I took some magical medicine and practiced directing the energy of belief daily, I could change my biology. We need to move away from the stigma the medical community has attributed to the word placebo, dismissing it as meaningless. Placebo is showing us what is possible beyond what we have considered to be true.

Back to walking along the rocks...

Limiting Possibility

Though I tried, I could not seem to repeat the experience I had while walking along the rocks. I was *expecting* possibility, and, in this case, the expectation itself got in the way of it happening. Expecting suggests the presence of someone doing the expecting, such as an "I" for example. In this case, "I" was in my own way, for when I was walking along the rocks, I remained in simple awareness—just noticing.

If we truly wish to manifest possibility, it seems best to not do so from an ego state. I think being open to all possibilities, seeing each moment as filled with capacity, is an exciting way to exist. It is manifesting all possibilities without effort. Being *hopeless*, the opposite of being open, manifests possibilities that are more aligned with hopelessness. Our openness impacts what we can experience as possible, which can be negative or positive experiences.

Earlier I suggested the possibility of pushing the envelope of our understanding of what is real. If someone is open and starts to experience psychic or paranormal events, does that suggest reality is paranormal at times or only for that specific person? Each of us are grounded in our own understanding of reality, per our unique life experience.

Often, when loved ones die, the deceased may visit the grieving. They lovingly drop by to let us know they are okay and often present exactly as they appeared when alive (even though in the afterlife, they no longer have such form). When this happens, those who experience it take that extraordinary moment in, casually, as if it were an everyday occurrence. They know that they are with their loved one and feel comforted. There is no freak out—it just is. And each event I have heard about, including my own experience with visitation, is that it is simply, unconditionally accepted. No one says, "Oh, it was my mind playing tricks" or "I imagined it." They simply accept it with the same level of calm as we might accept that the sun is shining. Yet, if someone connects with Christ or an angelic or extra-terrestrial entity and shares it, we question, scrutinize, and judge. We assume that is not normal and therefore must not be real, that they are lying or imagining, and we just cannot trust or accept their experience of reality. This hypocrisy illuminates our bias regarding what is possible.

If we suspend this bias, we see these ideas that have been established as "the way things are" block us from greater possibilities. These ideas are married to how we self-identify. We don't just self-identify via our historic narrative of who we think we are. Our collective narratives have defined realities attached to them, including what is real, not real, and limitations on what is possible.

I have noticed that chemical dependency is linked to our implicit memory system. And by using EMDR Psychotherapy (a memory-based therapy), this dependency can be switched off in one session, terminating both cravings and withdrawal. This removal of dependency now challenges the alcohol gene theory that suggests a genetic cause of addiction. I have done this over several years with hundreds of people, and it has a 100 percent success rate with people who complete the treatment. But when I post on social media or addiction blogs, I am viciously attacked, called names, berated, and even accused of propagating harm. I only post a new possibility without denying what we already know, not attacking what others believe or embrace. They could read my post and take it or leave it, but instead, they feel threatened by the suggestion that what has been for the past century is about to change. I am not saying I received this information from a Martian who dines with me every evening. They act out because this clinical approach yields a seemingly "impossible" outcome, as such results have never been seen before.

What if Louis Pasteur was discouraged from growing mold on

watermelon to create penicillin? Or better yet, what if Michael Jordan was told he was not good enough to play basketball in high school? If he did not believe in the possibility, he would never have become a household name. Limitless possibility is not limited to the Michael Jordans of the world. It is there for us. We just need to step out of the way.

The Ego Lens

The ego includes the I or Me part of us as well as a system that filters our experience before we receive it. The ego protects us through this screening and, if necessary, will selectively distort what we receive. Thus, ego protects us by distorting our personal reality via this filter system, which creates historic experience.

For instance, if my parents often shame me and seldom validate me, I will grow up with a distortion (or filter) of never being good enough. I don't apply for my dream school and settle for the safe choice. I don't go for the raise I rightly deserve. I settle for a spouse who is just okay, as the person I really wanted to marry feels too good for me. This protective filter keeps me from thriving and taking positive risks. These negative or limiting ideas feel real, and we identify them as attributes of who we are! But if we can look at our beliefs about who we are, our preferences, and how we have defaulted to these ideas, we will see that we may be restricting ourselves.

What if I don't engage this idea of "I"? I need to think to be an I, so who am I before thought? I cannot answer because I need to think, to use language, but let's cheat: I can feel my body sensing without thought. Without thought, I sense, I smell, I feel, I taste, I see, and I hear. I may also just know (intuition). I know I am alive, as I can see that and feel my body breathing. I can turn my head at will and move my body. If not I, who is breathing? We do not have language for that. The I that thinks in a self-identified manner feels different from the I who experiences breath.

For sake of discussion, let's say the I that thinks in a self-identified manner is the Egoic-I. The Egoic-I is the way we are raised to identify, as a separate self, separate from others, as well as things like the dog, the room, or even the air in the room. We must think to be an Egoic-I, as Descartes said, "I think, therefore I am." Egoic-I identifies in separateness because we each have our own story about who we are. Identifying with this historic view is why I like vanilla, and you prefer chocolate. We have a history with tasting both, and now know which we prefer. The Egoic-I, however, screens experience through that history. As with the example of not being good enough, our distortions can be in thoughts, emotions, ideas, and even senses. Often, we are not aware of such filtration regardless of when it is experienced internally (as an idea about ourselves) or externally (distorting what someone said or how someone spoke to us).

The war veteran hides under the table when a balloon pops at his 5-year-old son's birthday party, as that explosive pop is associated with danger in his Egoic-I's filter system. If we are an I or a Me, we risk experiencing our world through a distorted lens; that you are separate from me—that separateness which you experience is also a distortion. Ideas of possibility are limited by the distortions of our Egoic-I. The idea of an egoic self is just that. We think I-ness is real. It is a concept that cannot exist until we think. We can breathe and beat our heart without thinking. Do we not exist?

Right now, put your pinky in the air and wait until the skin on your finger tells you which direction the air in the room is moving. Be patient and concentrate, and it will come. This shifts your brain to awareness so we can discuss being egoless. Notice how quiet your mind becomes without all the (Me) chatter. Notice if you are calm.

We exist as a non-Egoic-I, experiencing itself, being in the world we perceive before us. I experience the light in the room, the seat I am sitting on, my feet touching the ground. I can feel the air grace my skin ever so gently. The air gracing my skin is not filtered. It directly transmits tangible, unbiased information about its presence around me. That experience of air is exactly as it is and has nothing to do with *me* as egoic or separate. I am not separate from the air touching my skin or floating invisibly around me. The air is part of my experience of being in a room, as is the light, the floor, walls, ceiling, and other people. I cannot separate from the air, the light, or gravity holding me from floating to the ceiling. In fact, as I inhale the air, my body is using the air in the room to make more of me. I exhale molecules of me that become part of the air. I am interacting sensorially with all these experiences at once, and they are inseparable from my experience of them.

We develop the illusions of the Egoic-I and grow up to believe it's real and that it's the whole ball of wax. Personal identity and individuality offer a safe, assured view of the world—a sense of separateness that provides order and convenience. And yet, all of these can be achieved without a separate, egoic self. In fact, positive risks come more easily when they are not fighting these egoic filters.

From a non-egoic view, I am not separate. I am one with everyone and everything before me. Still, I am diverse. I am different from you, but as you read this, these words share the experience of my own mind. My thoughts live within you, are digested by you—if only for a moment. Our thinking continues without self-identifying. It is not separate—only different. You may disagree, and I respect your individuality. However, you experience me now through my thoughts and writing, which are inseparable from you at this moment—that is a non-egoic lens.

If you feel confused or a bit off center, know this is a normal reaction to solid, long-standing beliefs being questioned. If you look up at the sky tonight, ask the stars to go away and prove you are separate from them. You and the universe do not exist independently, though the stars may twinkle more than you. They are different—not separate. As these ideas sink in, you may notice you think without being a separate *I*, without using thought to self-identify or service ego.

In short, the ego, or separate self, uses emotion to assert its presence. The Egoic-I teaches, through these emotions, how to navigate the world. If I experience fear, I shift course to stay out of danger. If an old fear arises (a filter), I must learn its source and release it, so I am no longer afraid when no dangers exist.

Rancid helps us stay safe and learn. We discern what is real and when we are stuck through the sour taste, even though it feels unpleasant. We use the Egoic-I to learn, feel, and honor what is rancid. In recognizing this, we can free ourselves of any filtration (or distortion) that does not serve us.

Discernment of old and new enables us to learn from the filters by feeling them and exploring their sources. Clearing out these old filters allows us to be present and begin a new level of learning and evolution. As a trauma therapist and in my own healing, I have noticed that after the "big stuff" is released, finer releases become apparent in layers between increases in energy. The energetic experience of being comes from our soul. As the mask of negativity lifts, we finally begin to experience our *soul-self*. We feel energy and increases in strength and frequency as we evolve. Possibilities expand when we move beyond limiting filters.

The Filter System

While it is our Egoic-I that experiences these filters, they can exist before an ego forms in childhood as part of our defense system. As we age and develop ego, new filters can be created under its watch. Significant traumas, however, do not depend on who minds the store, as survival must always be prioritized. Filters are memory. We have many types of memory, and this type is designed for long-term storage. Long-term as in as long as we are alive, unless we do something about them.

There are two types of such memory. One is a type of implicit memory. It acts as a filter to be triggered by sensory input—screened by the thalamus—and sets off the brain's emotional alarm—the amygdala. The amygdala sets off a set of chemical and electrical processes that cause a physical and emotional reaction. If fear is triggered, we experience anxiety. If shame, over time, it will turn into depression. We can recall positive moments, but our implicit memory-involved defense mechanism prioritizes memories that are, in some way, a threat to our identity. The other way we protect, and store memory is through dissociation. This type of memory is reserved for more helpless, powerless, hopeless situations where fighting or fleeing is not an option. The memories are walled off from access or embodied to protect us from becoming overwhelmed. Embodied memory can be held as disease states commissioned to assist in protection (often as a form of immobilization). They can still act as filters, triggering anxiety, immobilization, hopelessness, and depression. They may also embed within the body.

There are two types of dissociation—one physical and one energetic. If I am helpless and about to experience emotionally overwhelming violence or sexual assault by someone who is supposed to love and protect me, I may have to leave my body to survive such. My *energy* body (our body has an engaged energy field around us) relocates to the ceiling, floorboards, or inside the wall until safety is re-established. The ensuing dissociated memory is stored energetically in our auric field rather than physically in the brain. The aura is part of our energy system—a sensory field that surrounds us and connects to our chakras, charged with processing energy as emotions. The aura resembles a sense organ and acts in our defense by expanding or, in this case, storing dissociated memory. Dissociated implicit memory usually resides in the brain, walled off from our awareness of such. It can also be held by the physical body. It may act up later in life as immobilization. For protective purposes, the implicit memory system sometimes shares memory with the body. Our soul also has access to remote memories, such as preverbal memories and being in the womb. It also has access to memories of past lives.

We can be overwhelmed with pain and dissociate- thus dissociated memories are manifested and destined for long term storage. When someone dissociates they check out. They seem present but they are not conscious of being at that moment. Partially leaving (partially dissociating) is called depersonalization, and is when someone is aware of being present, but experiences being disconnected from their reality, and cannot feel emotion.

When a child is not permitted to express anger, getting humiliated or punished if they do, the need does not get extinguished, though the expression of anger may cease for survival. The result can be TMJ or lockjaw. The body locks the jaw to protect us from releasing anger. We may outgrow the threat, but the body maintains our defenses until the filters dissipate. If we use hypnotherapy to release the anger held by the jaw, the body unlocks it. Fibromyalgia, chronic undiagnosed physical pain, repeating headaches, and migraines (if not associated with a medical condition) are all examples of the body expressing the implicit memory as a physical experience rather than an emotional one.

I had someone whose legs froze up in pain. Hypnotherapy gave her legs a voice. She asked her legs what they needed to say, and clearly, they said, "Stop! Stop what you are doing, and if you don't, we will shut you down." She had many debilitating medical problems, yet her family constantly assigned more and more housekeeping tasks, neglecting to see how physically frail she had become. Emotionally, she could not bring herself to say no to her sisters. As we devised a plan, her pain and stiffness began to retract. By the end of the session, she walked out freely with no stiffness or pain.

I had a migraine sufferer whose brooding boss triggered her. This transpired, as her boss reminded her of her evil stepmom—the true cause and source. After we used EMDR and hypnotherapy to release the implicit memories, her migraines ceased. This was just before she was scheduled to start Botox injections and magnesium infusions—both designed to treat symptoms but neglect the cause.

I have found that dissociated parts within so-called disease states were conditions created to help the person survive. Each person had hours of dissociated memory I processed with EMDR, followed by energy work to spark reversal of the physical conditions.

Special therapies like EMDR Psychotherapy and hypnotherapy can deconsolidate them from a fixed state so they can be changed and perhaps released from that special, protected status. In the meantime, we get "triggered" by these memories. Cognitive and verbal therapies are not able to do what EMDR and hypnotherapy can do because a part of our brain, the amygdala (our emotional alarm), protects these memories from being changed.

Trauma-specific therapies work because they get past the amygdala. We need to be aware that our ego distorts reality via these filters (implicit memories). We sense danger even when we are safe. We hear rejection when that is not what was said or intended. We settle because we think we do not deserve better or are not good enough. We must serve others first, or they will not like us. If we see a spider, snake, bee, or some other creepy creature, it will sting or bite us, and we will be in severe pain and possibly die. When we look in the mirror, we see ourselves as overweight regardless of what we weigh. If we have never been loved, we can never learn to love or be loved. If we have been abused by those who were supposed to protect us, we can never trust anyone—ever. These are all egoic distortions. Fear is the greatest teacher. However, fear can creep into many areas. Fear underlies distrust. It is the core of experiencing scarcity or betrayal and abandonment. Fear is easy to notice and feel and serves to protect. Our job is to see if fear is still needed. Is it an overreaction to what is present? What can I learn from fear? What of this fear is not true—or is no longer needed?

We coexist with ego, using it to identify feelings that point to challenges we now welcome. We welcome challenges because now we know they are lessons to help us grow and ascend in our path to knowing who we are as a soul—in oneness with Source, Love, Light, or God.

Our soul also holds memories beyond this current life, and sometimes, as part of our processing, a past life comes into focus. It often shows meaningful parallels to what is currently being explored. Sometimes we taste rancid, and it feels like a part of us, but we cannot figure out why we feel what we feel. Sometimes a déjà vu sense accompanies such experience, though not always. Souls take on our human form to learn lessons via our lived experience, and this is part of an ascendance/evolution process. This happens when our soul feels we are ready to learn lessons from past lives, usually during or after we process and release lessons from our current lifetime.

Now let us examine another part of the brain's operating system that enables us to experience being—awareness.

Chapter 2

AWARENESS

Awareness is an operating system using parts of our brain to be in the world, much like ego, only different. Our experience of awareness is the world as it is, unfiltered or distorted. Awareness serves up our worlds as truth. It is a bigger, more expanded view than ego, which believes we end where our skin ends. Viewing the world with mindfulness and becoming aware of this interconnection may help us navigate the challenges we face on the individual, group, and global levels. We may bypass the fear-based thinking associated with the trials of the world today and, with our new knowledge, help to shift humanity to a higher consciousness. That may sound pretty high-level, but let's start with the simple process of mindful awareness and its operation in the brain to ease our way in.

THE AWARENESS LENS

We have established that the brain has two operating systems. Now, let's move to the outer cortexes to explore the world through the lens of awareness. We switch between awareness and ego hundreds of times per day without knowing. As we now step into this operating system, you will learn to discern which you engage at any given time.

The idea of the Egoic-I does not exist in awareness. Mindfulness training helps us move away from this domination ego has over us. Mindful awareness is simple. We all already engage in it daily, though we may not be aware. Awareness is easy to put into practice. The challenge is sustaining it, and this takes practice, time, and determination. As we practice mindful awareness, the associated neurons begin to wire together, and it becomes more natural to simply live in awareness. You can literally hardwire awareness permanently in your brain with practice over time.

What is *mindfulness*?

It is simply noticing the present moment.

We discussed moving into awareness by simply raising your pinky. You feel the air *now*. Your heart beats *now*. You breathe *now*. This is reality, where real life is lived. There is no *I* judging the air or filtering the information you have received, as in ego states. It is as it is, and you can only know which way the air is moving at this very moment. It is a direct experience. Notice that the feeling of the air on your finger has nothing to do with who you are. It does not matter how you self-identify, as no concept of I(Me) is required at this moment. Expand what you notice to the room or surroundings, noticing textures, colors, and sounds, both near and far. Notice the neutrality that prevails; everything is as it is. It is neutral. Just being. No chatter in your head—it's quiet.

We can notice our body: what we experience inside when we breathe, what needs to move to make that happen. How does our experience of our body change when we become angry, sad, or happy? How does our posture change when we feel afraid or strong? We can be in awareness (noticing) or in an ego state (self-referencing, feeling, forming opinions, judgments, and referencing history or the future).

We commonly switch between our ego state and awareness. Think of walking through a doorway to the world *within* and the world *without*. Can you notice when you are in awareness (OUT) or engaging ego (IN)? At times we may be doing a little of both. Notice when in different situations whether you are IN or OUT. See if you can notice switching. "Catch" the switch. See if you can deliberately switch and switch back—walk in and out of the doorway.

You can ground highly charged emotional states by noticing how you experience emotions in your body. What is your breathing like, your pulse, how hard is your heart beating? What muscles are tightening? Are you sweating? Notice where you physically experience this emotion in your body and just stay with it, continually noticing that sensation until it dissipates. If you stay with noticing the sensation, it will dissipate but may take a while. Be patient and focus on the body—not any thoughts or feelings. Sensing is neither feeling nor thinking.

We can go outside ourselves with awareness to *ground* as well.

Try this: Assign yourself awareness tasks such as noticing room corners, textures, and colors. Notice five round things, five soft things, five blue things, five sounds, sounds near and far, etc. Notice the color of someone's eyes, the texture of their voice. Notice the silence. See if you can find shadows. Are they warmly-colored or cool? Do the edges change in shadows as you follow them? Notice what direction the air moves across your skin. Can you feel the air at the tip of your nose? On top of your ear? Eat a Red Hot™ or something extreme that would be difficult to not notice. Smelling lemon or lavender is known to have a calming effect, but noticing subtle senses of smell and taste can demand attention and be similarly effective. Effort is the experience of the brain moving resources from one place to another, to where we are trying to notice something subtle. It assures a change in the direction of awareness.

The "Flow" process, you will learn, uses deeply focused awareness of the subtle energy in our body to take us out of ego state. Once we practice moving between *ego* and *awareness*, they become easy to discern.

To summarize:

Ego:

Separate I(Me)

- Distorting filters (memory)
- Identifies by history, evidenced as memories
- Memories and emotions validate a sense of reality, can be experienced as suffering
- Beliefs are often self-limiting, as ego is protective
- Thought required
- Ego occupies the limbic (mid-brain) system and frontal cortex (front of brain)
- The present is filtered by our past
- Ego is experienced as past or future tense or reference

Awareness:

- No *I* needed nor present
- No filters, no history; experienced in the moment
- Neutral, not emotional; personality is preserved
- Thinking optional, not self-referencing [I(Me) conversations]
- "We are not separate from all that is"
- "I am not in my own way, can take positive risks, think in a limitless way"
- "I am expanded to what I experience, not restricted to the illusionary boundary of my skin"
- Awareness is in the outer sensory cortex, outer brain, and surrounds the limbic region

Compassion

We can more easily feel pity for someone else who suffers, than we can feel it for ourselves, but neither helps in our pursuit of practicing compassion. Self-pity involves feeling sorry for ourselves, but compassion does not. Pity involves feeling sorry for others, but compassion does not. In self-pity, the Egoic-I feels sorry for itself as a separate individual, thus pity for someone else also suggests separateness; "I" feel sorry for "him" (her, them). Self-pity engages suffering and just brings more suffering, as it resolves nothing.

Compassion arises as an urgent need to respond to suffering. When we offer compassion, we send a wish for healing to occur, for the pain suffered by that individual or group. We take charge and help resolve the issue, or we feel a genuine understanding. Compassion occurs when we are in awareness, noticing others.

During the holidays, ads by animal shelters manifest compassion by displaying suffering animals. We feel compelled to act, write a check to that agency, and/or rescue that animal from helpless neglect. Compassion does not come from Egoic-I. It comes out of an awareness in which we do not experience separateness. Thus, we notice the suffering of others, as we are not self-focused. Automatically, compassion arises, and we want to do something about the suffering.

Compassion is intolerance for suffering.

Compassion can be an unconditioned experience. We may experience compassion with no reason or cause for it to manifest. Conditioned experience predicates itself on a cause. *I am happy because I got paid.* The happy emotion depends on the act of getting paid. Most emotions are cause dependent and thus conditioned experiences. Being in awareness is an emotionally neutral state. However, if we were suffering emotionally and are now neutral, we experience the absence of suffering, which feels good. It is still unconditioned because no action or cause was needed. If you experience compassion, it means you are noticing others, and that is a good thing. That is why it can naturally arise out of *awareness*.

To practice self-improvement, we must responsibly remain in relation to *all*, as opposed to a separate Egoic-I that judges what is. If I judge myself, I will suffer. I then can have self-pity. Or I can be in awareness and unconditionally accept my actions. No judgment or suffering. If I am already suffering, I can have compassion for my suffering ego. People will struggle with self-compassion, as the separate Egoic-I says, "I do not deserve to not suffer."

This is an important lesson, and the suffering connects to an idea we learned a long time ago. Ultimately, we will learn that our "non-deserving" was learned from being deprived by caregivers. It was about them and their acting out—not about us. We did not cause a life sentence of deserving to suffer. Learning this releases us partially from the irrational belief, but we also may need to process emotions and somatic sensations to release it completely. The Egoic-I will protect this idea that we don't deserve love or compassion, as it possibly saves us from a worse, more painful idea—the idea that if I am neglected/abused, I am therefore unlovable, or that my parents don't love me, as their behavior suggests this. That feels far worse, so the ego decides to self-blame rather than accept the idea of not being loved. I would rather be broken and unlovable and believe they love me than realize a more painful truth. I rationalize that I must have been *really* bad for them to treat me as they did. Egoic-I protects the lie until the truth is revealed by investigating and processing this situation. Being able to have self-compassion helps us mitigate resistance to such, expanding our awareness of what I may need to investigate and release. What we need to become aware of, to "let go of," are *lessons*.

LESSONS

The ultimate purpose of being human is to learn lessons and evolve, even if it happens through challenge.

If we could reframe life challenges as loving lessons, they would be easier to rationalize as a less painful way to approach adversity. Our challenges are lessons that exist so we can learn, grow, and evolve. There is a reason such challenges exist. We can then pull back and see this not as arbitrary or coincidental. I refer to this plan as our *Divine Plan*.

When we recognize we live within a Divine Plan, *Divine Flow* manifests as an awareness that "what needs to happen" is being laid out before us. I call it Divine Flow, as it feels like everything flows perfectly into place. The universe provides perfect lessons for us to learn exactly what we are ready for at that time. Our lessons may even serve to prepare us for future lessons within this life journey. We expand our awareness and realize everyone works within a Divine Plan, and the world we engage in is perfectly part of that plan. There are no accidents. Meaning and purpose exist in all things that happen, including all traumas, atrocities, and loss. We may struggle to find such sense or meaning in our experience, but from a higher view, it is available most of the time.

Our soul's journey does not begin with our birth. It may have had many human births as well as many non-human births prior to ours. Our soul lives beyond birth and death. Our soul is eternal—it does not die and knows no fear, let alone fear of death. Our greatest fear as a human is the fear of dying, yet if we distill who we are down to realizing our soul selves, there is no fear. We realize our eternal existence. Emotions are energy and vibrate at different frequencies. Fear and shame vibrate slowly, at lower frequencies than the energy we feel and realize when we connect to our souls. Our soul exists at a high frequency in which fear cannot manifest because fear belongs to a lower frequency.

Human Death, Soul Continuance

When we physically die, our soul leaves the body and goes through several levels as part of crossing over. Leaving the body serves the purpose of experiencing healing and more opportunities to learn with the result of evolving further. Being in a human form is a medium through which our soul can take on an evolutionary nature. We will first experience healing and then be assisted with a life review so we can see what we have accomplished in our life plan and what we still may need to work on. We have contracted to attain learning during our time as a human. The progress will be shown, though not as a karmic scorecard with judgment. Judgment requires ego, and no egos exist in the afterlife. Rather, we experience an encouragement toward self-reflection on how we may have chosen differently. Opportunities present to further repair areas that will further our evolutionary progress. This includes a period where we can influence or in some way reconnect with those we have left behind to manifest such repair.

We may need to apologize and may do so by making something in that person's life easier. We may use dreams, nature, or symbols to leave messages. Often after a loss, people report visitations—the deceased, in visual form, manifests to visit in a dream or in waking life. I referred earlier to how, when it is experienced, it feels natural and normal. In the afterlife, we will exist in a higher frequency, so insights will be easier to realize. Everything is focused on moving forward, on evolving as a soul toward realizing oneness with God or *Source*. That may mean taking on another human life to work on agreed upon-goals in a new "life plan," and we may be asked to be in service in another capacity rather than taking on a human incarnation. For a deeper understanding of afterlife, I suggest Lisa Williams's *The Survival of the Soul*.[6]

We need to realize that everyone is a continuation of a soul, as it does not cease at death. Our deceased loved ones stay in very close proximity to us, yet most of us are not aware of it as a common occurrence. In my practice, I do not directly act as a medium for my clients, though I have had many experiences with the afterlife and beings who have passed. I instead help those struggling with loss to connect with

---

6 Lisa Williams, The Survival of the Soul (Carlsbad: Hay House, 2011).

their loved ones so they both may complete any unfinished business. This is powerful and often easy because people who grieve carry the energy of their loved one with them in the form of their grief. This energetic calling card makes it easier for them to connect to those who have passed. The connection almost always happens because if someone thinks nonstop or feels deeply about this person, they already have that individual's attention energetically. These are not arbitrary connections.

My mother expressed her love through cooking. She was an excellent cook and often made everything from scratch. We enjoyed her ethnic dishes, and she glowed as we expressed appreciation with moans of joy after each bite. On occasion, I will pull out one of her recipes and share my mother's cooking with my wife and children so they too can experience her gift. I can feel the connection with her as I manifest her continuance. I experience her when they take their first bite and throw an approving glance in my direction. I experience love as she did.

One day, I took a mediumship workshop and, in the afternoon, partnered with a total stranger who was charged with connecting to the deceased person I wanted to connect with. We were instructed to bring something belonging to that person, as it had their energy. I gave her a recipe card in my mother's handwriting. This person took the index card and deliberately avoided reading it, as to not be influenced by the writing. Soon after, she connected, said *your mother is here*, and announced what I cooked the night before—even though she held an entirely different recipe in her hands. This confirmed my mother's presence as I cooked and sensed connection with her.

Cooking as an expression of love is one of her continued manifestations, though not in the human form familiar to us. If my children express love through cooking, my mother's continuance resumes, and perhaps on to their children, and then their children, and so on.

We do not die when our human form is no longer viable. We move on, and our connection to this plane may resume through a continued presence and/or through the continuances we leave behind. We are infinite and eternal. Realizing this helps us in identifying with Source, or God, who is love, both infinite and eternal. As a soul, we too are love and both infinite and eternal. God is the master *Creator*. We, too, are creator beings and create all that we experience.

Past Lives: Lessons via Soul Memory

Lessons can be learned from past lives shared by our soul, who holds memories of all its lived experiences—both human and prior to humanity's existence. We can use hypnotherapy or direct soul connection to visit a past life and explore how that parallels a lesson in this lifetime. I struggled with an issue of scarcity and was prompted to take on a past life journey.

As I crossed the threshold from this timeline into another unknown time, I stepped into the body of a nine-year-old Black girl in a field harvesting cotton. A sharp pain shot above my left ankle—a leg iron had cut into my flesh, as it was far too small. The cotton plants stood tall, towering over me. A scratchy burlap bale hung over my shoulder. I was sweating in the heat, and flies landed all over my face. A dark feeling of grief overwhelmed me. It was my father. I learned he was just killed by the man hovering over me, who sat on a horse with a gun and cowboy hat.

I was not allowed to grieve. I had to keep working, or I would be killed as well.

The young American enslaved person's name was Anna Brown. Anna's soul (my soul) chose to grow up in a life of extreme limitation and suffering so she would be forced to look elsewhere for freedom. I knew I was in this memory to learn a lesson, so I asked young Anna to fast-forward me to another chapter later in her life.

The scene refreshed, and now I stood before a twenty-something young woman with a scar running down across her skull. Anna hated slavery and learned if she resisted her enslavement, she would be met with more suffering, permanently maimed, or even killed. She had no option but to walk through suffering even though she did not know where this path would lead. Realizing her newborn baby was born into a life of bondage; she felt that pain and compassion as she held her child. She told me, recognizing I was witnessing this moment, to come closer. She wanted to show me that under the pain was love and compassion for her baby, who was just beginning an entire lifetime as a slave. She noticed and continued down that path. She coached me to come with her, deeper and deeper into her consciousness as love. Love without condition or limitation—love that was infinite and deep. She experienced a love that could not be contained. She realized she *was* love, and so was the child she held. She was experiencing life through a different lens. In this place of love, she kept expanding. She whispered to me, "There are no shackles here." I physically shook as I took in her words. She realized neither the iron around her leg, or any other awful physical abuse or limitation, could stop her from realizing the limitlessness within. She realized learning the permanent truth of being a soul—one with source, one with all that is, why she was a slave. Slavery taught her to look inward, as engaging or resisting slavery was eating rancid food.

Experiencing the limitation of scarcity, my soul prompted me to do a past-life regression to experience limitation and meet Anna Brown. Anna had already done all the hard work, and I feel so grateful to her. Anna realized her role in this life was to experience freedom. She manifested an external world of extreme limitation (rancid tasting) to be prompted to look within and evolve.

My first past-life regression was in April 2017, when I regressed all the way back to the beginning of time. I experienced myself as creation. I was a massive galaxy giving birth to another galaxy. It was stunning and mind-altering, an out-of-body experience that I knew had deep, life-changing meaning. I knew someday I would understand why I experienced this. I was ready to experience it but not ready until now to understand it. We create our experiences based on what we need. I, even later, also learned this was a past life of part of my soul, as Archangel Metatron helping to create the Universe. My soul had chosen this memory for me to experience and witness. I later would get its meaning and implications. I even used the memory and energy as part of a later lesson in ascension.

Ways We Can Learn Lessons

Now look at your own life, the family you were born into. Look at the relationships you have manifested at work and with family and friends. What is your situation, and, when you pull back, what can you sense you are being asked to learn? Do you have pain or an illness? Look at what it keeps you from doing. What do you need to learn to move beyond suffering and struggle? What challenges do you wrestle with? Are there lessons that originate from when you were very young that are re-manifesting now as an adult? If so, it is because we have not learned that lesson yet, and when it is learned, our reality will shift to reflect that. You will manifest that shift! You are a creator being and a master in manifesting! When we can realize this, we can pull back and take charge of this projection we call our life. We can more clearly understand the life purpose laid out before us. We will see that we manifested it so we may embrace the pain and suffering as teachers.

Loss can also be a teacher. Our life plans overlap with others. We learn from each other—that is not an accident, nor is it arbitrary. Sometimes those very close to us must leave as part of the Divine Plan they agreed to. Their death may seem untimely—after all, when is unwanted loss timely? We may pull back after our grief and explore what purpose this leaving may have served. That person's leaving may also be about helping us move forward on our lessons by taking what we learned from that relationship, from that person, and seeing how we view it now that they are not here before us. How are we enhanced by their leaving? That may sound offensive or disrespectful if you are not ready, thus I suggest grieving first. Grieving is painful but incredibly healing, as it is an expression of the deep love we have for a loved one. It helps us say goodbye to the relationship and let it go. The person is not gone, but if we choose to continue to relate to that person, it will not be the same. That person-to-person relationship is over, but they are still very much a part of our lives, whether we are aware of it or not.

I mentioned the person earlier who suffered from migraines and had an evil stepmom. Her loving biological mother died suddenly when she was only five, and her father remarried soon after. Her new stepmom had forbidden her from crying or grieving the loss of her mom and removed all pictures of her biological mother. Her inability to express emotions (grief from loss and anger for being emotionally restricted) resulted in a physical manifestation (she was forced to eat the rancid food) and thus manifested chronic migraines. After processing the trauma of this event, I could sense the longing to connect to her mom. I know that when someone thinks and feels about a deceased loved one, their presence is nearby. I asked if she wanted to connect, and, after affirming, I helped her to finally express how she felt to her biological mom and to lovingly say goodbye, though decades later.

Such connections can change grieving so that we can focus on the lesson needing to be attended to. It changes the healing process. We do not feel so mortal when we connect to a person who has crossed, as that affirms our own soul's continuance. Experiences can be a vision, voice, or gentle touch. It may be a knowing. Sometimes people get full sentences. Other times, just a sense of presence. Confidence that afterlife exists can change our current life. Do I need to resist death so much if I am at my life's end? Perhaps I can let go more peacefully, knowing I only end one experience of being to begin another. I can release my fear of death, and perhaps not resist so, when it is time.

A way to experience afterlife, and lessons from afterlife, is through past-life regressions. These are done by a guided process using hypnotherapy or via our soul showing us directly.

I will show you how to connect to your soul later.

Some teachings about cutting the chords of negative past life experiences, so we do not carry the karmic debt of that past lifetime, are not true. We may be learning contracted lessons that were not completed from a prior life, but we do not carry karmic scorecards. There are no such scorecards in afterlife. We are not judged, but lovingly encouraged to learn, grow, and evolve. I have learned these lifetimes are precious visits into our soul's history, and we go through them to learn that those past lessons are usually parallel to what we currently go through. Cutting chords prematurely denies us a special, rare, and sacred opportunity to learn a lesson shared by our soul. Cutting chords, those connections to past lives allegedly plaguing us, was a method taught where I learned clinical hypnotherapy. I now understand this is disregarding the truth and denigrating an offering through divine guidance. It comes from not wanting to taste rancid, and our soul does not want us to suffer but to use suffering to learn. Our soul is in divine alignment. We do not want to ignore any prompting or offer to share by our *Divine Self*.

I have had several past-life regressions, including one in which I followed my lifetime into afterlife as a survivor of the Hiroshima holocaust. I knew I had been a survivor of this, as I suffered nightmares of such for two years—particularly through the nights of August 6th. I practiced a standing Qigong mediation during the year in between the nightmares, but on the second year, I opened the newspaper to a picture of a mushroom cloud: August 6th was the anniversary of Hiroshima's atomic bombing. I jumped and felt as though this information was shared with me for a reason. Twenty-seven years later, I decided to visit that lifetime and learn why I needed a deeper knowledge of it. These past-life visits take you back in time, and the experiences are both amazing and life-changing. They have so much power because they are memories of our soul—memories that allow us to witness and learn.

Such journeys will ultimately help us apply lessons to our current challenges. These past selves are all *me*. I embrace these memories as my own. Now, my soul and my soul's *human incarnate* share memories together. Many of my initial regressions were not earthly experiences, but intergalactic.

Our soul has had many incarnations, and not all as humans. We can learn from all our soul lets us see based on what we are ready to experience.

Our soul holds within it our "Akashic Record." The Akashic Record is the name given to everything our soul knows and has experienced—time forward and back without limitation. When we experience past life as prompted by our soul, we get permission to access information from the Akashic Record, this sacred resource of all that is known.

Some have suggested the existence of karmic debts that are hung on our lifetime for repayment, as if in judgment. Much has been written about the relief felt after exposing past lives where very bad things took place. There is no such judgment, and every opportunity is provided compassionately in afterlife to help us learn lessons we missed during our lifetime. In Andy Tomlinson's book, *Healing the Eternal,* he suggests we reincarnate to provide opportunities to resolve unresolved Karma in prior lives.

If important lessons critical to our soul's evolution still need to be learned, they can be added to that soul's "goals to achieve next." It is necessary for our soul's highest interest, but not as punishment. The physical pain or emotional challenge we experience, which may be related to past lives, is our soul offering us a chance to learn through processing these regressions.

DIVINITY WITHIN ATROCITY

One of the most significant experiences of my past lives relates to what

I do now—in this lifetime—as a trauma therapist.

This was the life as a survivor of Hiroshima during the atomic bombing. It was the life I experienced just prior to my current life.

When I stepped into the body of the Hiroshima survivor, I immediately felt overwhelmed with emotional pain and horror I have not experienced in my forty years of practice in trauma therapy. I knew I would step into a traumatic memory before I undertook this regression and thought I had prepared to weather this storm, but I had no clue what this would be about nor how important it would be to my own transformation.

Information flowed in. I knew, from dreams, that I survived with my elderly, dying father. He needed water, but none could be found initially. Only when it was too late did we learn the water was poisoned by the fallout. The whole city was poisoned. I realized in seconds I had lost everyone I knew, except my father, including friends and family. I lost my job, the buildings where I worked disappeared. I lost every reference point of who I was. Nothing that existed before was the same—just death-like skeletons and shadows of city dwellers and family, who, in a flash, were ripped from existence. The pain I felt grew rapidly and could not be contained inside my skull. I felt my insides ripping apart. It was unbearable, but I forced myself to stay with it. I physically shook in horror, as I had descended into a nightmare worse than any horror film, worse than anything I have ever experienced. I spent time with this self and lived his brokenness as we moved through his life. He moved from despondency to guilt for having survived to just being numb. He survived with others who were broken too. No one was unscathed. I—as him—had no reason to carry on, but lived out my life, longing for the day I would die, to hopefully be relieved of my suffering. I was fifty-nine when the bomb dropped.

I renounced God, for how could God allow such to happen. *No, there could be no God; that was all a myth*, I told myself. In my current life, I was not raised with any religious training and had never developed a concept of God, let alone a relationship with God. I even avoided books that mentioned God, as that term elicited nothing but confusion for me. At this point in my development, I experienced high frequencies (*energy of being*) and situations that had me flirting with an idea of what God is—at least experientially as energy. Still, I was able to understand the renunciation of the presence of God in the Hiroshima past life, given the horrific trauma.

As the survivor, I asked for death to rescue me. I noticed there was no resolution within this lifetime to an overwhelming situation, so I decided to follow this life into his afterlife at age sixty-five, to see if there was a lesson. I know past-life regressions are about lessons, and this was no exception.

At his death, a tube of light came down, anchored by two spirit beings encouraging me into the tunnel. I followed it into light and found myself in a pod-like container. I felt exhausted, drained of energy from that lifetime, and I could not move. But as I lay there, a flow of energy surged through me, both healing and energizing. It was a delayering process assisting my transition into afterlife. I am not sure how long I stayed, but, after a long while, I moved into another room. Surrounded by other souls, or light beings, I was given an opportunity to review my life and life *plan*. I became outraged and protested. "How dare you ask me to review such a life? Are you going to question whether I appreciated life enough before the bomb, and so here is my big life lesson?" I spoke—sarcastic, loud, and very agitated. Others rushed in and helped escort me out to a different room. I was not ready for such a review. They placed me in another room where I could continue healing.

This was different.

The walls were pure energy, and there were no ceilings (there is no weather in afterlife). I saw a pipeline traveling out of the room over top of one of the walls to a place far away. The energy being piped in was, at first, calming and soothing. My pain and anger melted away. Then the energy shifted and became a higher frequency. It kept morphing higher and higher, and then thoughts started streaming in. I was connected to God! The energy lifted me toward realizing him. I started to realize the bombing of Hiroshima were actions of man—man created and dropped the bomb—but the extreme horrors were the design of God. Yes… God.

An atrocity happened in Hiroshima. If it was atrocious enough, man would never resume using this weapon, threatening Earth's existence. It had to be terrible beyond anything we could conceive. Only God could manifest what was needed to save the planet given an event so threatening. But he did so lovingly. The pain served as protection for the planet. It was necessary to save Earth from annihilation. I learned in the afterlife I *volunteered* to survive, along with countless others who volunteered to even be sacrificed, to save Earth. All agreed in advance.

Meanwhile, the energy increased constantly and became overwhelmingly intense. I was becoming one with God. As I realized this, my current self-experienced the energy as abounding and too intense to fit inside me. I became so overwhelmed with bliss that I could not tolerate it increasing any further. Like the trauma—equal in intensity. I decided to opt out of the regression and opened my eyes. I had two energies outside the front of my head. On one side, the trauma of Hiroshima. On the other, realizing oneness with God. They were experienced as two file folders in an energetic form.

I walked around for two weeks with these files that were too big to fit in my brain hanging out in front of me. They were equal in size and intensity. I was no longer in the regression, yet there were these files to be reconciled as my lesson. I needed to merge them, but now, each by itself seemed too much to handle. Two weeks passed before I could sit with each. It took a lot of work and many meditation sessions to finally assimilate the merging of these two experiences. Once I did, a whole new shift into a steady state of higher consciousness occurred. I have no doubt the lessons from this past-life regression played a major role in knowing who I am as a *soul*.

I could now see the relevance to my practice as a trauma therapist.

It may be controversial to frame the Hiroshima atrocity as *divine* or as the work of God. I am not blaming God for Hiroshima. God only intervened because man chose this path of destruction. But let's look at other examples where atrocity, being that rancid taste, presents itself to help humanity and the planet stop choosing such horrible paths.

WAR

I have worked with war veterans, and their experiences are no less horrific. They witnessed buddies be disemboweled and killed in the same way *they* have disemboweled and killed an anonymous enemy. They have realized they are no different from the enemy they were forced to kill. Both were contracted by governments far from the front lines of battle. Decisions to engage in warfare were political decisions that had little to do with reality on the ground. The causes each side sacrificed lives for had no impact on those doing the fighting. The extreme distress (rancidness) caused by war (rotten food) stays with survivors, whether they're soldiers, civilians, or animals, for the rest of their lives. But the *horror* of war is necessary.

It is incongruent with supporting life and evolving as a human collective. We are discouraged from committing war, as it costs far too much. The atrocity of war is the real price, and it is so we, as humanity, will hopefully learn and never ever forget. Why do atrocity makers like Bashar Hafez al-Assad, the President of Syria, have documentaries made of his war crimes? He had photographers document all the fatal torture applied to the fellow Syrians he oppressed. Pol Pot of Cambodia and Hitler both meticulously documented the ethnic cleansing and genocide they undertook. Creation of a legacy may have been the intention, but this documentation of horror provides a lesson we must attend to: *Do not blame God for the suffering war must create.*

Man chose war and genocide in free will, not God. On a personal level, the soldier survivor may initially renounce God. Who could blame them after living through such hell? They will see their role as heroic or helpless. And within the context of a bigger picture, a shift occurs. As we pull away, we see that we are no different from the enemy that attacked us or who we attacked. If I killed someone and could connect with this faceless being, could I ask for forgiveness? Would this being accept that offer and perhaps offer an apology for the harm they caused or lives they may have taken?

When we equalize the separateness of us and them, we move into the diversity that is within *equanimity* (we are different, but the same). From a higher perspective, we both stem from "Source," but we may have different skin color, hair, eyes, beliefs, gender, etc. I may wear a different color uniform and be on a different team. But we are all in oneness in our diversity. We are all human. Both the enemy and I, as the soldier, have been thrust into this traumatic experience together. We have the same job as soldiers. We eat the *rotten food*, we taste its terrible taste, and we get spiritually sick from the experience. Heroically, though, our soul agreed to have this experience for the sake of greater humanity. This is a lesson contracted before our soul took us on as a human incarnate.

Personal Atrocities

In my practice, I attend to lives that have been traumatic, some since birth. Suffering does not need war to be present. It does well enough within dysfunctional family systems. When I help individuals release their traumas, I help them realize the underlying lessons or truths revealed as to who they *really* are. The meaning of their lives shifts and when all that work is done, they can use hindsight to see that who they are now is because of what they learned. They realize the *divinity* (truth) within their personal atrocity.

I worked with a Purple Heart war veteran, and we processed a war scene where he felt deep fear for his life for a prolonged period. As his fear desensitized from engaging in the EMDR process, we stopped to ask what he was taking away from the experience as a life lesson—as a new truth? I asked him to go beyond the obvious: *War is hell.* He suggested *appreciation* emerging from feeling safe. This person is very sensitive because he is in a deep awareness of appreciation. He has very profound experiences, loving music and family. He realized he was gifted this through his horrible, frightening experience. He could not afford to appreciate anything while in imminent danger presented by the presence of an enemy he could not see (it was nighttime and dar, walking thru the jungle). The silence he experienced was deafening.

He would share YouTube videos of his favorite pieces of music. He described how listening transformed him; his face would shift, as if deeply in love. This could only emerge from feeling safe in contrast to the endangered silence.

Darkness defines light. His soul gifted this to him so he could realize this higher truth. Our soul is love. We do not feel our soul's love like we feel human love. Our soul is *divine* love in which we realize rather than feel. The difference between feeling and realizing is that, in realization, we know that we may also feel.

Sometimes the lesson does not seem clear. It may be difficult or even impossible to see. We may not be able to know the lesson until a later moment in life, as there may be other parts or people involved. In my past life as a survivor of Hiroshima, the learning and realization did not make itself available until afterlife. Our understanding is based on readiness, and we are privileged with insight and knowledge when we are energetically ready. We shouldn't judge ourselves or others for not initially understanding certain lessons. I may know that rancid taste points something out for me to explore. It may be a terrible life situation. Or I may not understand the connection it has to me in this lifetime. I can know that recognizing this has been lovingly manifested for a higher purpose. It may be helpful to imagine the terrible event no longer exists. What would be different about how I regard myself? What would I do differently? How would my decisions about life shift? Can I take those decisions and apply them now, in this context of terrible? Sometimes by exploring such differences, we can discover what the lesson is.

Our dense reality deliberately shields us from the truth of knowing who we are as a soul as we age. This veil seems irrational. We want the good stuff now. W*hy should we have to wait and work so hard?* The veil sets us on our way, undistracted to engage in free will—to act out our challenges, failures, and ultimate lesson breakthroughs.

Could there be a better way to do this?

What if we already understood that we are souls manifesting a life of lessons and challenges for the purpose of self-realization? Would that create an incentive for us to do "the work" and stop spinning in place? Perhaps we as a humanity are ready to know this. Or perhaps some of *you* are ready. I posit the need to trust not knowing so we can surrender to truth, and at some point in our journey, we will arrive at the information we need.

We do not contract our way into a human incarnation in a vacuum. We have a "Soul Family"—those who we incarnate with lifetime after lifetime. We enter our life with contracts with others who will enter our world at birth or in later chapters of our story. They help us experience lessons—good and bad.

There are times when we have been hurt and may need to forgive. We may have been born into a family contracted to provide us with enough rancid food to almost kill us. Forgiveness helps us move on.

Dissolution of Separateness

If we watch the news, we see states or nations acting in a protectionist manner, which is coding for racist agendas that blame others. Blaming is a way of not taking responsibility.

It is a deep spin on separateness. I know others have felt sick from this kind of news event, and we can see those actions against the environment or against personal freedoms make us feel sick. The urgency of wanting change manifests this sickened reaction. It is a lifting in consciousness. We learn and discern from the foul taste what is or is not congruent and aligned with our divine nature.

We become sickened by separateness, and we need to pay attention. We need to realize we are not separate from each other, nor are we separate from the disease that afflicts us or even from the planet we live on. Animals and plants do not engage in separateness. They live in an interdependent harmony interrupted only by the actions of humans. The living and breathing Earth has been exploited and victimized because of human separation from it. Free will allows us to discover our own individual path in self-realization—not to destroy or exploit like this. There is no *us* or *them*. We are both us *and* them.

We *are* the Earth, not separate from it.

Try to separate yourself from our planet. Separate yourself from the sky at night or the stars. The ground you stand on is shared by your friends and family. It is shared by the rest of your town, province, and country. It is shared by those you love and by those you consider enemies. You are sharing the ground with all inhabitants at once. It links you. Your idea of being separate at this moment is just a thought—an idea. Its illusion is revealed as the truth emerges.

We are not separate from Earth, and Earth is not separate from the solar system. Our solar system is not separate from our galaxy, the Milky Way. The Milky Way is not separate from the universe, which is not separate from the multiverse. Just feel the expansion from ego to universe, and it should lift you energetically. Here we step into an expanded view of who we are.

Let's take it further.

Within our physical form is energy. Included is love, which has an unlimited range. This love energy belongs to a super high frequency, existing as our soul-self and living on within us. Our soul veils itself from us until we are ready. As we are readied, glimpses bleed through, we know things, and we feel a more blissful energy. It prompts us to act or learn lessons that move us closer and closer. This is Divine Flow.

In realization, our reality expands to all that is. There is no separation, and rancid cannot be tasted, as rancid vibrates at a much lower frequency. At a higher frequency, we can see rancid and rot, but we cannot feel it. We can see others suffering, but we cannot feel their pain. Suffering and pain belong to very low frequencies. We use our Egoic-I to taste rancid and experience suffering. When we see someone suffering or someone perpetrating suffering on another, we judge the situation in an instant. We taste rancid and need to separate to be safe and to avoid identifying with the threat. It acts as a defense mechanism that prompts us, unconsciously, into ego, so we can judge and thus separate. We can get stuck in judgment—usually expressed as anger—which can be a catalyst for change. Or we can pull back and understand we are not separate but do not need to align with the rancid before us. I do not need to dance with someone who will hurt me or eat that which is poisonous. I can use suffering to learn what causes the pain so I can work toward change that removes the experience of suffering. In this view, suffering is vital and acts as a catalyst to saving us. We can go further and say suffering is sacred, as it asks us to ascend from separateness.

When we talk lovingly as we hold a baby in our arms, the baby will break out in a smile as if it smiles with its entire being. We immediately feel joy, a physical cascade of good feeling flushes through. Scientists say natural opiates produced in our brain facilitate this experience, triggering a release of endorphins and dopamine. We want more. We do it again, and it quickly becomes addicting. This natural bonding assures we will continue to attend to our young with the love and protection they need. This happens without fail in the animal world, provided the young are healthy and will survive.

It fails to occur in humans about 20 percent to 40 percent of the time, resulting in addiction, health issues, depression, and anxiety. The failed attachment then replays generationally unless someone gets help and breaks the cycle.

If you examine your life right now, are you in this cycle? What part do you play? Can you buy out of it? Are you experiencing the love that makes you want more? What challenges do you engage in? Can you see the lessons beneath those challenges?

- How would your life be different if these challenges never existed?
- Examine what excites you versus what you hold in fear. Is your fear old, perhaps even ancient, or triggered by some event or person?
- Can you learn from diving into this fear and engaging in what it wants? What is the opposite of this experience? For example, if you fear being alone, how would it feel to not fear being alone?
- Can you get to awareness and see this through that lens? Notice how it is different.
- Can you empower yourself to change—is there enough urgency? Is there someone you know who can help you be empowered to shift, or do you need to find a coach or a therapist?

Our awareness of our situation, including our dilemmas, is where we start. We cannot start anywhere else, as this is where we are, the current moment in which we inhale and exhale. As you inhale and exhale, can you add to your awareness the idea that you are exclusively, energetically responsible for the moment you experience, unconditionally and without exception?

You may say: *Woah, I can step back to view my life, but taking responsibility for creating it? I cannot wrap my head around that!*

In Zen Buddhism, one path of teaching utilizes Zen koans—questions or sayings that cannot be answered or responded to with thought, as they are beyond thought. Instinctually, we attempt to think our way out, but this fails as the teacher nods with disappointment. The koan shakes us from our automatic response of thinking. So, this idea is perhaps from a view that is too high a perspective to comprehend, but the thought that it could even be possible shakes us.

Let us look at a simple example for clarity.

Let's say I am depressed and in a relationship with someone who makes me feel unworthy. I decide to move away, and I notice I feel better, not having unworthiness triggered. I decide to explore further, and, in therapy, I learn that my family was the source of this trigger while growing up. I release the trigger as I realize I am not unworthy and never was. It was their inability to treat me as I needed and deserved, and I experience a shift. I feel even better and notice the people at work respond to me differently—they become nicer. The ones who treated me poorly don't come by, and I do not accept if they are not nice, immediately calling them out on their inappropriate and unnecessary interaction. I learn to limit contact with my family, as I realize they do not know how to be respectful. I begin to attract only those who treat me well and enter a new relationship with a wonderful loving person and feel so happy. In hindsight, I see that I was born to realize my worth. My soul chose for me to learn this via the family it selected for me. Having failed to learn worthiness in my family growing up, I attracted people in my relationships and at work to treat me as unworthy until I could no longer tolerate the rancid taste. I decided to stop eating the *rotten food*, as it made me depressed. Learning my lesson, I moved away from the rancid experience wherever it manifested, as I no longer needed it. I did not need to manifest such. Instead, I start to attract people who see me as I truly am—worthy and respectful—and treat me as such. I also see the worthiness in others, and this expands me and feels good. I can see others struggling as I did and now have empathy for them.

My energy has lifted me to where I can see much more. If I were lower down, I would be stuck with the details of what is right in front of me, and I would be too close to have that pulled-back view. As I elevate energetically, hindsight becomes clear, and now I can see my lesson and how I attracted what I needed to prompt me to learn it and move on. What I needed did not feel good. But if it did not taste bad, there would be no urgency to change and thus learn. The rancidness provided urgency to change. I changed my experience by moving away from suffering. My world shifted. The people engaged me differently. I no longer saw suffering as an option in the new world I created.

We can see that we energetically vest, create, and change the experience we used to believe we were separate from.

Our soul manifests what we need to know, where we need to be, what we need to learn and experience to perfection. We and our soul are one. The awareness of being in the world manifested by our soul dissolves boundaries of separateness. It is like a dream: We are all the parts in our dream, as we manifested the dream. It did not come from someone else. It is all ours. It is all us. The same with this awakened dream we call our life. It is us.

It is being conscious.

PART II

EXERCISES

Chapter 3
COPING AND HEALING

To process the negative experiences we carry and heal from their physical consequences, we may employ several different methods. These include ones I use within my own therapeutic and personal practices, ones taught by ancient civilizations, and ones that you may carry with you throughout your day-to-day life. Regardless of your background, these exercises may assist in raising your frequency and resolving your separation and fear-based challenges.

WORKING WITH ENERGY

By understanding energy, we can change our emotional state instantly.

In this chapter, we will practice a technique I developed called "Flow."

The first part quiets the emotional, thinking brain in an exercise referred to as *rapid grounding*. The second part gives us remote control over our emotional state and allows us to switch to whatever emotional state we choose. We may need to feel safe, loved, courageous, inspired—the choice is ours and the change takes place almost instantly. Sometimes we are too emotionally activated to effectively achieve Flow, as it requires us to concentrate deeply. In that case, do the "Pause" section first, which I will describe below, followed by Flow. Pause is also a rapid grounding tool.

As a rule, energy listens and responds to intention. Intention drives the action in Pause. Focus your intention and allow the instructed actions to be acted out.

Pause

Emotions and pain are energy.

When you feel emotion in your body, you manifest its presence as energy. If you have strong emotions, drop into your body and bring these feelings there. Notice the spot where you feel that emotion strongest. With one hand, try to vacuum and grab the emotion with your palm (intend to grab all of it) and scoop it all into a tight fist. Hold it there. Then dramatically rip it out of your body (with strong intention—don't just *take*). Do not open your hand until it's far away from your body. Throw the energy across the room. This emotional timeout provides you with as much time as you need to *ground*.

Now that the greater quantity of emotion is out, if you check in, the feeling should be gone. If you still feel a little, repeat the action as many times as necessary to completely clear the negative energy. This will work on physical pain as well. You can test it by trying to reactivate the distress, and you will find you are unable to after several Pauses. It does not sustain for long, and in a short while, this Pause exercise will need to be repeated unless you pair it with *Flow*, which has a longer ability to sustain.

Now try Flow.

Flow: Rapid Grounding

Sit with both feet flat on the ground. Bring your awareness to the bottom of your feet and notice a tingle inside the arch at the bottom of each foot. You may not notice that sensation right away, as it is extremely subtle. Just deepen your awareness by exclusively focusing on that spot within your foot, and the tingle will magically manifest! It is always there; we just need to notice it. Sometimes we need to patiently wait, but this is only a matter of a few moments. Once you notice the tingle, move your awareness to your ankle. Notice a similar sensation there. Once that sensation is felt, move to your calves. This will be more like a gentle pulsing, flutter, or pinging. When you notice that flutter, move to your thighs, feeling for the same sensation. Once you notice the sensation in your legs, continue to your arms then spread your awareness to your abdomen and chest. Eventually look for similar sensations in your neck and head. Notice the vibration now in your entire body. Hold your awareness on these sensations and, at the same time, briefly notice how active or inactive your mind is.

Your mind should be very quiet, as it must shut down to enable you to deepen your focused awareness to sense these subtle vibrations. The vibrations are the normal bioenergy running through your body. After you have some practice and you know what to look for, your body memory will assist, and you can scan your whole body and feel all the subtle sensations at once. Then try focusing most on where you *don't* feel it. It will be a quicker process.

We are 60 percent water and run many functions with electricity. Thinking, moving muscles, breathing, beating your heart, to name a few, and these subtle sensations are your electric current. The quiet will sustain, so enjoy.

You are in deep awareness. Come back to your body.

From here, you can launch into meditation or move on to flowing.

FLOWING

Now create an intention to make this energy move downward, from the top of your head to your toes. Imagine a stream flowing through you with a waterfall to the ground at your knees. You will soon feel the energy moving. When you have established *Flow*, notice how it feels.

We can now change the frequency of the vibration.

Imagine pouring a bucket of bright yellow paint down your stream so that it is flowing yellow. Your entire being is flowing yellow. Notice how the vibration has shifted and how the vibration of yellow feels. Now pour light blue paint down your stream and notice how light blue feels. Notice that light blue has a different vibration than yellow.

Try flowing an emotion now. Just as you poured paint down your stream, you will now pour an emotion down. Notice the vibration of that emotion flowing down your stream throughout your body.

Imagine you just received a phone call from someone you have not heard from in a long time. You are surprised yet delighted to hear from this person. Imagine how you might feel emotionally. Perhaps some low-level excitement mixed with a warm feeling deep within. Just notice in your body how this sensation feels. Notice the vibration it has and flow this vibration down your stream. Let it flow through your entire being.

Now let's try flowing love.

When you mentally reference love, use loving a pet over a person unless you have an example with a person who has no negative baggage attached. Notice the vibration of this emotion and let it flow down your stream. Feel it flowing through every cell in your body. Notice how the sensation feels. Feel how different this vibration presents and how quickly we can change this vibratory experience. Let's make this feeling stronger.

Let's flow *divine* love.

Imagine it is stronger and more intense. Imagine *this* love is radiant and glowing love in all directions, warm and luminescent. Flow this radiance down your stream. It may feel warmer but allow yourself to experience the bliss that manifests. You can stop here or continue as a meditation. If you start to tear up or cry when flowing love, note that feeling is the act of grieving what you may not have had when you were younger. Allow yourself to feel this grief as it connects with another form of love—healing.

You have the freedom to imagine whatever you wish to feel and flow that by tapping into the experience and noticing the vibration. Flow it down your stream.

You are in control.

You are not only taking charge of your emotions, now you are playing with energy! We can flow calm, courage, inspiration, or, if in physical pain, endorphins as anesthetic. If it's not strong enough, just imagine flowing a stronger dose. You see we can flow whatever we want and change our emotional state to one we want. Instantly.

Flow as a Healing Tool

We can use Flow as a vehicle to flow healing energy as needed.

I once practiced Flow with someone who had just been diagnosed with breast cancer. It had not spread to her lymph nodes, so I suggested we try. She flowed healing energy, and it went straight to a spot under her arm where the cancer was located! While she proceeded with a medical plan and had the tumor removed three weeks later, she practiced Flow daily, and it gave her a sense of control over her condition, feeling like she was doing something about it rather than feeling frightened and helpless.

What would have happened to the tumor if she did Flow more frequently for a prolonged period? Would it have shrunk or disappeared? Would it have been healed through the power of placebo? If so, we see how applying principles of healing via placebo design may be about directing energy to heal or allowing God to do such healing (in my meditation sessions, I have channeled that only God can heal).

I had six people who suffered symptoms because of COVID-19. One was paralyzed on her left side due to an autoimmune response flaring up. When we practiced Flow, the energy immediately went to the left side of her body and started working on her joints. It became intense and even uncomfortable for the person, so she stopped it. It was clear, however, that this energy followed the orders of the intention—and meant business. When COVID was just blossoming into a pandemic, an ER nurse who contracted COVID-19 tolerated the energy more easily. It remitted her symptoms one by one. First, she felt the tightness in her chest release. The energy focused on her sinuses and brought back her sense of smell. Then, she could feel her fever stop. Her energy became lighter, and she no longer felt fatigued. Finally, she felt all her aches and pains release. I suggested she continue to do this three times daily, and she did. One week later, I checked in, and she reported her symptoms had not returned. This was before any vaccine or COVID-specific treatments were developed.

I have repeated this successfully with several others with COVID. What other healing possibilities might Flow be a vehicle for?

Working With the Merkaba

Our energy body consists of layers of *aura*, a field surrounding our physical form connecting to energy centers known as *chakras* that metabolize energy for our physical body. These chakras can accumulate debris from life and may not always function properly.

Our body comes with a very sacred dime-size cleaning tool, the *Merkaba*, prepacked within our solar plexus chakra. It looks like this:

Our solar plexus chakra is three to four fingers up from our navel, and if you bring your awareness deep within, you may notice a subtle buzzing. If you do not notice this at first, just patiently maintain your awareness inside the center of your body and it will present. This three-dimensional form spins rapidly clockwise but horizontally (your left to right). Once you have noticed it, it activates and can now be directed to clear all your chakras, starting with your root chakra at the base of your body. Send it (using intention) to the root chakra to begin clearing. Feel it drop to the floor of your body and begin working. It will automatically move from chakra to chakra until it's done. Amazingly, you will feel it working and will get to feel each chakra. Sometimes it will move in a linear fashion to each chakra, such as going from root to sacral, then solar plexus, then heart, throat, third eye, and crown chakra. Sometimes the Merkaba jumps around, and that is fine; we just let it finish up at the crown atop our head. Once there, ask it to go as high as it needs to clear the chakras in the etheric layers of our aura (two above and two below). We then ask the Merkaba to scan our aura, and you may feel this. It may show you things that need attention or healing. When done, we move onto healing. We call in the Medical Assistance Program (a spirit team) to scan and heal us as needed and to clean our Merkaba. The Merkaba will return to the solar plexus where it lives. You will feel energy coming in. Let it run, as it will heal whatever needs attention. You can suggest things like, "Please work on my right shoulder," and the energy will attend to it.

I know "Medical Assistance Program" or "MAP Team" sounds strange, but there are two different teams. One is the Universal Medical Assistance Program, and the other is a Personal Medical Assistance Program. I have tried both and see no difference in efficacy. The "Program" refers to energetic geometric designs to manifest healing they may ask us to hold. If you are coming off a trauma history, it is especially beneficial to run this Merkaba clearing/healing, and you will notice the difference. If you have a chronic medical condition, it may take many more healing sessions to effect change.

I used energy to get rid of my bone spur, in my shoulder. In the xray it was a finger-like bone petruding from the joint. Removing that required daily energy work—30 minutes daily for over six months. I have no sign of it now and do yoga without restriction in mobility.

Energy listens to intention, and this is key to our present and future lives.

Combining Flow with the Merkaba to Heal

Combining Flow with a Merkaba, we can possibly advance healing—reverse disease states, remove bone spurs and cysts, grow endocrine tissue, increase bone density, reverse inflammation, and speed recovery of almost any malady. Flow is utilized to provide the source of energy to which we attach our intention. The Merkaba contains an energetic blueprint of our DNA in *energetic* form. For healing to happen, this intention must be made with 100 percent commitment and belief that healing will occur. We must be all in. There cannot be any doubt present regardless of how extraordinary the healing. Do not give up. Healing with energy can take a long time. Be patient, committed, and persistent.

Next, imagine taking your Merkaba and placing it over or around the area in need of healing. You can use multiple Merkabas, and if you need one for your whole body, just imagine a Merkaba big enough to climb into. To potentiate healing, ask the MAP team to help. This is rarely a one-shot, but that also depends on the situation. I felt a tear in my shoulder while gardening and placed a Merkaba over where I felt the injury. I held it there for twelve hours, and it hurt even more during the healing, but there was no sign of injury after the healing duration.

Energy healing can take months of bathing an area in energy for a minimum of thirty minutes daily. I believe combining energy, intention, and a Merkaba has the capacity to do miraculous things, and I speak from personal experience. Add MAP team aid as well, and you have serious healing potential. A Merkaba can be used as a vehicle to access an earlier time (hypnotherapy can be used as well). We want to access the Merkaba prior to a disease state and bring it back into the present. It is that Merkaba that is then applied to healing via intention. You can also simply intend to use the DNA from a healthier time. The Merkaba contains energetic DNA, so all the information needed to repair or grow new tissue is there.

I present a very simple model for applying Merkabas in healing. I need to add that a Merkaba is extremely sacred and vastly complex. Reversing disease states is very complicated in that it means possibly identifying dissociated parts of self, releasing dissociated memory, and asking the soul and the dissociated part if they are ready to do this healing. Healing may not be possible if there are contracted lessons related to the physical condition needing attention first.

If you feel depressed or present but disconnected (depersonalized), it is because you are energetically stuck in Dorsal Vagus (overlapping the lower chakras). Here is a link to video on my Youtube Channel of exercises that will lift you out of there energetically, switching off depression and depersonalization for as long as three hours www.youtube.com/MIbNkPl_9lk?si=f89uFKDRTg19FzX4.

Healing may necessitate other considerations, such as nutrition and exercise. When we look back on what we are healing, can we look deeper and see why we manifested that condition? Did this have a meaningful purpose for manifesting? Was this a result of surviving or negotiating a state that we resisted, as it was uncomfortable, or worse—intolerable? If we could become aware of when we resist being or when we do not resist, we would learn these moments feel significantly different.

We call a lack of resistance "Being in Flow."

BEING IN FLOW

Flow (not the exercise but the concept) is our ability to recognize challenges as life lessons and not resist them. If we accept our challenges, even if emerging from trauma, by releasing those wounds, we will learn things about who we are, and that will help us lose our attachment to the Egoic-I.

I'm on the path to knowing who I am as a soul.

If I know that I am on a plan to evolve, it is easier to accept my challenges as necessary. The Egoic-I will resist, as fear puts us into ego, and ego holds on for dear life by telling us this divine stuff is all a bunch of bunk. But, if we can get to awareness and scan our reaction to our struggles, we can objectively see this may not be about me, but rather what I learned through experience. Resistance as a knee-jerk reaction to rancid needs to be sorted from rancid itself. We may need to slow down and sort out our emotional experience. When we have completed this release, our frequency will lift, and Flow will be easier to identify. Release is most efficaciously done via processing in therapy.

Part of getting to Flow is raising our frequency—the energy level at which we exist. We feel the resistance and surrender it. Raising our frequency follows as we shift to a higher vibration when we feel good. Waking up to a sunny day off, listening to music we enjoy, being in love, cooking, creating, dancing, exercising, and especially meditation all demonstrate this concept.

I used crystals I could viscerally feel to introduce myself to energy. I brought those different energy flavors in as the subject of my meditation. You can do this as well.

Try this: Lie down and call in energy from Earth (use intention). Be open and feel energy from beneath you rise from the Earth. Be patient, as this may move slowly, but your simple intention will be enough to prompt its movement. Feel it moving through the backside of your body. Let it manifest and spread throughout. Then call in cosmic energy from above, coming in over the topside of you. Settle in and merge with the Earth energy. Feel this comforting vibration. Surrender, merge with, and be the energy. If you need to repeat bringing energy in, do so to refresh the energy experience. Just be. You are just being without resistance. It is being in Flow. What is flowing? At this moment: energy.

We accept whatever experience we come into as it is, without resistance. That is Flow.

Divine Flow is being attuned to our intuition and following what we are prompted to do. Intuitive guidance is from our Higher Self. It is a knowing, or "gut," feeling to which we surrender and trust. It is a path to knowing who we are. When we surrender to our Higher Self, things we need, including things we need to learn, fall right into place. It's almost magical at times, especially when we pay attention and start to notice this happening. That is Divine Flow. It rewards us with more if we surrender to it. It is our Divine Plan being revealed to us. You will know when this happens, as following Flow and the Divine Plan always feels good. Even though challenges laden with lessons may initially taste rancid, we soon know they have a positive intention as a lesson that will help us grow. I have found *pausing* after such a challenge helps. A day or two, sometimes a week, may be needed to step back and understand that this challenge is a message from our Higher Self or soul. Pull back and notice the big picture of what is taking place.

If we develop a meditation practice—say, thirty minutes daily—where we focus on feeling energy, we will progressively begin to feel the presence of energy post-meditation.

Awareness of energy as a steady state enables us to work with that energy and understand how it changes our view and our emotions. Emotions are embodied energy and are processed through our energy system, including chakras.

Working with God as a Spiritual Understanding

Are you uncomfortable with the word God?

You may have been raised to understand God as separate or wrathful and judgmental. Some religious institutions distort our access to God, as restricted to priests or religious leaders, for control over worshippers. Some worshippers have been referred to as followers, not sovereign beings who can access and be one with God or other Ascended beings. I have worked with an individual who was caught up in cult-like evangelical churches in the South, where sexual abuse of girls and women, if done by fathers, was condoned by the clergy as patriarchal culture and remained prevalent. That individual walked away with a strong aversion to spirituality and to any mention of God or religion. I have worked with several survivors who were abused by Catholic priests. This problem started as a local issue and became worldwide. Survivors left, distrusting the Catholic Church. I learned from survivors that the abuse was widespread, organized, and systemic. They were then left struggling with the belief system taught to them by the same people who abused them.

I was not comfortable with God until recently. I was not raised with any definition or relationship with whatever the world around me believed God to be. I worked steadily on my own ascension journey from 2015, and I have come to experience God through past-life regressions, self-realization work, and in first-person via my soul.

For those of you yearning for spirituality without an understanding or experience of God, be patient and know that a non-dogmatic understanding through experience can be realized through energy work. God cannot be defined, and if I attempt to explain God, I will fail. I experience God through higher dimensions within consciousness as energy, expansion, the culmination of very high frequency, oneness with all things, the realization of all time, all dimensions, and the infinity of space and being. I have met God, stood in the presence of God, and received energetic transmissions directly from God. I now have an ability to access a daily connection directly with God and know I am not separate from this experience. For me, knowing that I am in a Divine Plan and knowing that everyone is in a Divine Plan helped.

When I started to open to spiritual presences such as spirit guides, I started to have spontaneous visits by two very compassionate *Ascended Masters*, who decided to mentor me. They were aware I was a newbie at this spiritual stuff and had no sense of God. Visitations by Padre Pio and Mother Teresa came in tandem. Padre Pio, in very dark, heavy energy, has said, "All things are sacred. Every moment is sacred." Mother Teresa explained, "Sacred means *of God*." I made that advice a mantra, and I still hold it in the back of my mind. I have integrated those ideas and experience most moments as sacred. I am the experience of sacredness with those I am relating to or working with.

We are all sacred beings, each engaged in a Divine Plan to evolve through learning lessons presented as challenges. Even our health challenges are part of our Plan's lessons. We manifest what is before us through energy. We think a thought, which generates an emotion. Emotions are energy, and this energy manifests form. We are projectors of our reality. If we feel scarcity, we will manifest scarcity. If we feel fear, we manifest more fear. If we think and feel *I am love*, we manifest love all around us. We must release blocks to change energetically. If we are not conscious of this process, then we just need to accept that what we manifest is what we need, even if we are resistant to it. This is naturally difficult to swallow, but it is the purpose of this writing.

We may struggle with the experience of traumatic events when I am fighting to survive. We may move into a maladaptive way of coping with such experiences, and as this coping fails us, we may experience more pain (rancid taste). This lets us know that we have chosen wrongly and need to learn other options. If we have chosen correctly, we move in the direction of healing, not blaming ourselves for what happened. We learn that we are safe and capable, not helpless. We get to a place of resolution, and we are stronger than before, more aware of others suffering as we did. We are in a higher place because of our experience and the lessons we processed. We may notice we feel different, and people notice and respond differently to us. We are now manifesting a different world, congruent to the changes we have accepted.

If we step back, we can see that every experience helped us get to where we are. This lens we look through is not possible without all those experiences, regardless of how difficult the challenges seemed. The challenges are divine in function, as they direct us in a different direction. The function serves to protect us and help us realize how pointless it is to suffer. We need to be saved from ourselves at times, as the rancid taste of hating and blaming ourselves becomes unbearable.

It points to another option.

When numbing and avoiding no longer work, we must find healing, an option for our highest good. This is the Divine Plan. We can be grateful for being shown the nasty-tasting rancid food so we can learn to not continue to eat toxic stuff that makes us sick. Not a series of accidental, unfortunate events. Rather, a deliberate set of prompts to move us in a direction where we can begin to connect with and know who we really are. Ego embraces fear and uses it to exist. As we release fear, we get freed to walk away from egoic experience and separateness. Awareness of being free is higher consciousness. Gratitude is higher consciousness. Love is higher consciousness.

Immediately after the unthinkable terrorist attacks on 9-11, I noticed how our country changed. We went into a depression in the months following, which seemed to last about nine months. Living within proximity to New York, I worked with over one hundred 9-11 survivors. I noticed, beyond the fear and pain, that many were pausing to reflect, suddenly examining their lives differently. Life's meaning became important, considering the realization of our mortality that one day we may go to work and not return. People stopped taking their relationships and their lives for granted. Many people employed on Wall Street told me they were not returning to their lucrative positions in the city. "It's not about the money," they said as they searched for deeper meaning in their lives. The pain and fear prompted this mass introspection into our daily lifestyle. The daily mundane no longer felt acceptable, regardless of comfort. When people did this, it attended to feeling, not thought. We needed deeper meaning and needed to appreciate that we are just visitors, not permanent residents of this world. I am not for a second suggesting God created 9-11. That was a human act, but it is a clear example of how, when we go into the pain and fear, we discover deeper meaning and powerful lessons. The urgency in not returning to Wall Street, the urgency to seek life with deeper meaning are what we as humanity need to recapture. Urgency is required to make any change. We need an idealized target and urgency to energize movement. Can we manifest urgency so we can take on our challenges as lessons to create a more meaningful life?

We can build on this idea, as we do not live in isolation but in relationship to others who experience and work through lessons, flow states, and resistance, just as we do. Resistance can come from our history but experiencing each other as separate is often the primary source.

PART III

CONSCIOUS AWARENESS

Chapter 4
PREPARING FOR SOUL LENS

Surrendering to the flow and trusting that all may unfold in its due time is a practice that involves many facets, yet, with time and consistency, it may become second nature and elevate our lives entirely. Imagine releasing the fears and negative, false self-concepts that hold you back. Imagine trusting the greater plan through all of the toil and challenges in this life and navigating your days with a sense of trust and knowing that sets you at ease. It may sound too good to be true, but this reality lies within everyone's reach and can even assist in the greater universal mission.

INTRODUCTION TO CONSCIOUSNESS

As suggested earlier, consciousness is not in the mind (thinking brain). Consciousness is space and the awareness of the presence of being within that space. Imagine being a molecule of air. The only thing a molecule of air can do is just be. So just be! Now, let's add knowing. You know you exist, not as in intellectual knowing, but rather before thought, before self-identification. It is our gut response—we just know. You know through conscious awareness, which is awareness of being conscious. As a molecule of air floating about, just know you exist. Now allow this to be you in human form. I can just be in knowing. It is a very pulled-back view, a big picture of what is. The experiential global view of what is, including us, within that context of being. It is witnessing the awareness of being, not as an I, but as a molecule of air. We launch from awareness but surrender to this view by pulling back and being a witness to what is experienced. This is the view of being as our soul.

Consciousness Beyond This Life

When we are physically dead, our conscious awareness shifts as we leave our body. Our consciousness is now concerned with what happens in this transition between leaving a human life and crossing over to another dimension. We are not unconscious; we just do not have access to the physical means of expressing consciousness. Many publications document people who have had near-death experiences or have died briefly and have full recall. Mediums like Lisa Williams have explicitly documented afterlife from both firsthand experience and through communication with those who have passed on. I now hold memories of past-life journeys in my physical memory and have integrated some of those with my experience of being at present. I have had sixty-seven prior lives, and this is my last human incarnation. Knowing that makes this life especially precious. Holding such awareness of other periods of time and space shared with our soul is expansive. It is difficult to hold such memory and only regard my current human story as who I am. I am so much more than that, just from what I know of what my soul has shared.

I have already shared being a slave and a survivor of Hiroshima. Both were life-altering experiences, and as I went through those experiences, I knew my life was not going to be the same. During my first past-life regression, I was taken back to the beginning of time. I was not a human, but a huge galaxy. This was breathtaking, but then,

I birthed another galaxy of equal size. The energy running through this out-of-body experience felt indescribable. I had several other regressions to the Pleiades star constellation and to Cassiopeia and other stars and other dimensions, which were stunning, indescribable, and life-altering. Containing such expansive experiences, as well as the rich lifetimes my soul has experienced, created a new definition of being. I integrated my soul's experiences and soul memory as my own. It's certainly stretched my former ideas of being human! These experiences were all in a state of conscious awareness.

Consciousness is multidimensional (it exists at different levels of conscious awareness, differentiated by frequency). It is both vast and the vastness itself. Our soul consciousness always strives to evolve and never moves in reverse. It may be stuck or going slow, but it only moves forward. When we process negative experiences, it does not at first feel expansive or of high frequency. It does not feel like we are moving forward. It is being in Flow, as it is, helping us realize truth and release what is not true, what no longer serves us. We will lift in energy and lift in our view. Consciousness is bigger than we could ever imagine.

Surrendering to Get Out of the Way

I am worthy is a truth but notice *who* is worthy. *I* am. To ascend, we must surrender our new ideas of who we are—even ones we hold as truths. We surrender the attachment to ego that holds these ideas when the whole belief—"I am worthy," for example—is surrendered. When you have released these negative beliefs and other distortions, make a list of all these new affirmations of the new you:

- I am worthy
- I am good enough
- I am loveable
- I am confident

- I am strong
- I am authentic
- I am trustworthy
- I am in control
- I am powerful.

Meditate and hold this list before you (not necessarily exactly what I just listed, but your own personal, new, positive beliefs). Sit with these wonderful ideas, feel each of them, and own them. Then imagine surrendering them away! Surrender, let them go, step aside, and notice. Let them float away and dissolve before you. There will be space created. Don't rush to fill it. Releasing the wonderful, newly learned truths will allow us to move beyond ego. The truths will be unhinged from context and timelines they are associated with. Each has its own eternal quality. "I" has been separated from them like corn being hulled. We don't need the hull anymore. With experience in trusting the shifts in our world as we upshift energetically, we eventually reach a point of being able to trust letting go of what finally feels good. You may feel energy manifest. Of course, these truths are still present but do not relate to an "I" as we surrender and release the "I."

In a month, repeat the process as new definitions of self-manifest to fill the hole. We never entirely give up ego—we just ask it to join us in our ascension, and its role changes. It takes a back seat and, hopefully, agrees to stay out of the way. It continues its task of revealing the rancid taste of whatever new lessons may present. We release our *attachment* to ego.

True life meaning and purpose come with our emancipation of our soul from the bondage of suffering at the egoic level. The sense of freedom is celebratory, accompanied by a new urgency for purpose. As we peek out through a new lens, we experience our life redesigned. We must now acclimate to this new place; we notice our history now has less of a role. We change and now strive for new self-definition. We can look back, but now self-identification takes less priority in defining who we are. The need to define or redefine identity comes from the discomfort of emptiness created by this surrender. Definition, however, creates limitation, so it too becomes an obstacle to experiencing limitlessness. We need to surrender such definition and accept the accompanying emptiness. It helps to know we are moving to a place that is beyond definition, beyond limitation. Reframing is helpful, and those ideas sound more appealing than emptiness or void. We do not need to self-identify to be who we are in truth. We do not have self-identity in conscious awareness.

These concepts are not experienced as a moment where, suddenly, we get it and own it all at once. Instead, they integrate into our lives slowly and in pieces so we may be able to handle them effectively. The shifts subtly push that possibility envelope being held by our thinking, egoic mind. With each new realization beyond ego, we expand and lift in *conscious awareness*, experienced energetically.

Our egoic minds want to know everything, especially what happens next. When you surrender and enter a moment you have not experienced prior, the urgency to know what's next will be strong. This drives demand for the profession of psychics, as so many are willing to pay for a glimpse into a forward part of their timeline. These are suggestions of what we present energetically at the moment of reading, and we must understand that free will and following our intuition may diverge us from this suggested path. We ultimately will follow our Divine Plan. We will repeat what we have not learned and move to a new place if we have learned and processed our lesson. Needing to know what is next, as being in expectation, is egoic and often blocks us from moving or being in *Flow* and experiencing limitless possibility.

Ego's role protects us—like having an internal security guard. Knowing what lies around the bend provides us with an opportunity to prepare and guard against what may be coming. If we watch a weather forecast and a dangerous storm is predicted, we act in preparation. Thus, Egoic-I wants to know, even in good times. It takes us into expectation, and, if you are strongly determined like me, it is hard to turn such expectation off. In awareness, eventually we can see this is in the way. We need to realize we are still safe in not knowing what comes next. That idea is a great place to start.

Ask your ego security guard to relax, to realize it is okay and that you are safe. You may need to practice surrendering. We need to learn to be patient and step away from timeline consciousness as much as possible. This now moves into a territory we may not have experienced. It is unknown. We simply trust and *let*.

Trust and Letting

How do we accept what we don't know and trust that what we need to know will be manifested for our access?

Trust in not knowing is something I have personally found challenging, and it took some preparation, practice, and readiness.

Obviously, if we have had any trust issues in our lives, that is to be taken care of first. If I was abandoned, violated, or not protected by those charged with loving and protecting me, I learned to distrust to stay safe. After all, if no one is there to protect, I can protect myself by not letting anyone be trustworthy. I may have triggered wounds experienced by my caretakers when they were my age, and in this way, we manifest the lesson in trust. They became too consumed with their own stuff, neglecting to see that I needed to feel safe and loved. The distrust we learn serves us until we are older, bigger, and capable of our own protection. We want a close relationship, but distrust becomes an obstacle.

The lesson is realizing "I was always worthy of love and protection, but my protectors had issues that got in the way." It was not about me being unworthy or unlovable. I need to do deep work to release this mistruth and own that I am loveable and worthy of protection. I should be able to feel safe with people who have no ill intentions and want to give me love or support. We need validation that we are in the good hands of our Higher Self or spirit mentors, angelic guides, God, Christ, or others working with us, and to not be afraid. We may ask for validation of their presence, or for validation of something we asked for, as evidence we can trust. As material beings, we like things to be validated in that medium. The more we hold higher frequency energy, the quicker manifestations will occur.

Be aware that nature can be used to teach and communicate with you and provide such validation.

I experienced scarcity but had intuited that all would work out. Not trusting that information, I walked outside to find birds feeding their young in every direction I looked—on both sides of the street, on every block, in almost every tree! This was not a ubiquitous occurrence of bird nurturing, it was my Higher Self or spirit saying, *You are being taken care of and do not need to worry*. It validated what I already knew but did not trust. It was the evidence I needed.

When we sit on top of that urgent need to know, we sit on our ego.

Our ego will drive us to buy books, take courses, and divert us from just sitting in our *not knowing*. It does not like to spend time in the moment. Obsessing about what will happen next wonderfully distracts us from just being. But being open, in deep awareness, listening to our body and energetic presence is where information we need to know will be shared. We ask and are patient. We may need to direct our ego to "please take a seat and be quiet."

When the prompt to write this came, *I* wanted to know what I was to write; I wanted to know what I needed to know. I had to trust not knowing. I did not know I would be writing this at all, let alone as an entire book. I was prompted to type and surrendered to trusting the process that what I needed to type would present itself though the process. I do not need to know in advance what I am writing. I have done this with painting, so the process is familiar, only the medium is different.

Accept confusion as not knowing. Confusion is being off-center; it is because we are someplace unfamiliar. Unfamiliar is not safe, but we are taking a risk and trusting not knowing is okay. We feel confusion. Realize you are not melting into the ground like the Wicked Witch, and you will begin to relax. You are relaxing into a new paradigm. You are safe. You are present and open. Open your heart and crown. Receiving is a *letting* process. I do not need to know; rather, I need to be in Flow!

When we begin to lift the veil between us and our soul, we start to feel the love flowing through us. It can take some getting used to. At times, I have found myself tearfully overwhelmed with gratitude. Gratitude is a higher frequency, like love. We can use gratitude in mediation to raise our frequency. We just focus on being grateful for being loved and being love. We can extend that to the people and spirit beings around us who are supporting us. We can reflect with gratitude about all the lessons put before us, realizing this would not be so without those coming to a resolution. We can expand our sense of gratitude to being in a Divine Plan, to being in Divine Flow, expanding that to see everyone is in their Divine Plan, regardless of their awareness of such. They are in their process of knowing their true self, just as we are. We may be more conscious, but everyone has their own path. They have souls in oneness with God as we do.

Can you expand to be as one with God? You can use your imagination to assist with this idea. Energy does not know the difference between imagined and real, so if you imagine what being one with God is, you manifest and feel what you imagine as energy. Sitting in this expanded state, add gratitude. How could this wonderful experience be happening to me? It is because you are ready, and once the train leaves the station, there is no stopping your ascension. Be grateful and love-filled. It feels wonderful and sustains an increase in frequency.

We are always loved deeply, though we rarely recognize it. Angelic and spirit beings, members of your soul family of origin, Ascended Masters, and your Higher Self are all in a dance with you, either alongside you through challenges or in celebrating your humanity. They cheer you on, send love and compassion, and hope they may spark you to step toward their direction. They know you intimately and never judge. They accept you unconditionally, knowing you are working through lessons. They are with you when you are at the top of suffering. They feel your pain and know what you are going through. They want you to succeed but must respect your free will. In free will, choose to blindly accept this awareness, this assumption without any evidence. Surrender and trust that you are never alone and are loved deeply—always.

In meditation, I received multiple visits from both Padre Pio and Mother Teresa, as mentioned in the previous chapter. They kept tabs on me and would drop in to give advice or to prompt me to embrace some aspect of what divinity is. Padre Pio would announce his presence with this dark, serious energy. Mother Teresa would patiently wait her turn to come in, in tandem with her loving and compassionate energy. She'd say, "For you… For you," because she knew I was not raised with any notion of God and needed help with this idea. She evidenced that she knew me deeply and understood what I needed lovingly and without any judgment. I do not walk around experiencing Padre Pio or Mother Teresa, but I know they are intimately involved in my life, watching my every move, thought, and feeling. They are present, though I do not see or hear them. Honoring their assumed presence honors their love and divinity.

We can see that each moment is loaded with unseen support and love. Each moment overflows with more possibility that we can possibly know or realize. It is of God as we are, always engaging our Divine Plan to self-actualize whether we are aware or not. We are of God, so we are sacred, and our actions are scared. We were born sacred. We inhale and exhale sacredness. Now, we can give ourselves permission to experience this as reality.

Trust and let.

Breathing Exercise

Let us try a simple breathing exercise:

Breathe into your heart center by pulling air up from the Earth, through your root chakra at the bottom of your body, up your spine, and into your heart. At the same time, inhale through the crown chakra atop your head, down into your heart center. As you hold your breath there at your heart center, it will feel very warm. Hold your breath until uncomfortable, then release as slow as you possibly can. Slowly release and imagine the energy radiating slowly from your heart. Do this for at least eight cycles to feel this energy manifest. As you allow yourself to bathe in this energy, say to yourself, *Being is Sacred, I am Sacred.*

When you feel this warm, radiant energy, do you distrust what you feel?

Because it is three dimensional, it feels real to us. Yet, it feels good. When we connect with the affirmation "Being is Sacred, I am Sacred," we take a risk. We step outside what we have accepted as reality throughout our entire life and risk a new view. Just being sacred. Accept, even if it feels risky, and then try to do this daily for a while to get used to wearing this new article of clothing. Break it in and see how your resistance shifts. As you do this, notice from this energy how the world about you seems different. What happened to your wants and needs? Is there an expansion in experiencing who you are? Do not judge—just notice and observe. This graduated acceptance of shifting is learning trust.

Alcoholics Anonymous members are encouraged to attend ninety meetings in ninety days. This is what it takes to change a habit (we can change our brain permanently in twenty-one days). Thus, to deepen trust, we must be patient. Follow the rewards when stuff happens and do your best to not be in expectation. Expectation is of ego. "I" expect,

"I" want to experience trust. We let go of expectation by finding the moment and breathing into it.

Notice breath and come back to now.

It's okay that there is nothing happening now. That is providing space for something to happen. We join in the capacity of the moment and trust it. See each moment as pregnant with capacity and just be within. We are letting that pregnant moment give birth to whatever we need to know. We do not know the due date, but we do not need to. We just allow ourselves to be open and quietly trust.

Knowing and Truth

The new view we attain in this process may be looking down from very high up.

As we start to pull back and refine the presence of Egoic-I, Egoic-I becomes less important, though it does not leave completely. It is not the director of the show anymore. What is important now is everything and everyone before us. We see and experience what we manifested and co-created. We see and experience all as sacred. As if it were charged with a live electric current, we grab onto it and feel its charge. We are not separate from what we co-created, specifically for ourselves. We do not need to understand more than that. We are required to engage. No sitting on a mountain waiting for enlightenment. We engage the fabric of being, spoiled food and all, knowing every atom of what we experience is sacred. This is a truth that cannot be anything other. It has always been this way and always will be this way. It is the nature of truth.

Gratitude is another shade of love.

Love, as I have mentioned, is limitless in frequency range, multidimensional, and the single most vital emotion for our ascension. I have been overwhelmed by experiences of love throughout my life, for which I am grateful. It is in great contrast to clients in my office, some of whom have not been able to recall ever being loved by another human. The concept of love seems foreign and, at times, confusing. Yet those same individuals would not be at a loss as to what to do with a puppy if I placed one in their arms. They each admit they would hug and snuggle with the puppy without any confusion. They can experience the unconditional love this young life innocently offers, and it prompts them along to love back. I do not work with live puppies, but it would be great if that were not inconvenient. We see that we all know innately what to do—how to receive and give love. Our soul knows this, as our soul *is* love.

We may have learned love only exists with strings attached. Yet we all know we want to be loved, and we need to be loved. If I suggest to that person that they just love themselves, they look at me like I just spoke a foreign language. But if I connect the adult self with their inner child, love flows like holding a puppy. We all have the capacity to experience love and unmask the beliefs that stop us from experiencing this. When we can play with feeling loved, we can move to being love. Paul Selig's *The Book of Love and Creation* is a handbook offering instruction on moving into this "I am love" state. I am love, as energy, is very high frequency. It realizes the nature of our soul, at the same time realizing all souls are love, regardless of the human personality's ability to express such. The love of our soul is infinite. That is a truth that I cannot speak to, as it needs to be experienced. *The Book of Love and Creation* introduces us to this idea and provides the ability for us to taste this frequency, realizing love has tremendous healing potential, as it defies all egoic identities and attachments.

Only when fear and doubt are completely absent can we realize truth with unconditional resolve. It is a knowing that is beyond the human incarnate that you are. Truth is not a point of view or an opinion. It is a realization of what is not just before us but beyond us as well. The truth extends beyond what is known to what is unknown. How can I know that? Wouldn't that be impossible to know? Our minds have limitations, and knowing is not a mental activity. It is an intuitive activity that has no limitations. Thus, I know truth's boundaries must also be true beyond what is known. I do not know what will happen tomorrow, but I know I will experience whatever I need to experience. *That* is a truth beyond what is known. I feel this in every atom of my being. Our goal is to be authentic, to live in truth. That is highly idealized, but we need not make this too complicated. You will know intuitively a truth as it presents—we have those "ah-ha" moments. We just know and may even say, "I knew it all along!"

Knowing is not a foreign idea or experience, even if we've never actually connected the dots before. We may not be practiced in discerning thought knowledge from intuitive knowing. Some of the ideas in this body of writing, like how we manifest what we need to experience and learn, will first be received at an intellectual level. We attempt to metabolize the idea in our thinking minds to make it make sense. We may even feel a resistance to the idea at first, as it seems crazy to think about having some remote responsibility for a painful situation. When we pull back and look at this, taking off the Egoic-I glasses, we see what is possible. It begins to make sense on a *knowing* level, not an intellectual level, as it is not an intellectual concept. I can sense the situation will release and shift if I can understand what the pain wants to teach me. I need to be open. If I allow the fear and doubt to process out as the lesson resolves, I can realize intuitively what is true. My reality has shifted. I cannot doubt that, even with my thinking mind. Oddly, when we begin to have truthful realizations, it feels like it has always been that way. This odd feeling of knowing something new, yet also knowing as if it has always been, is referred to as *remembering*.

We are very old as souls. In my first past life regression, I saw creation. I cannot put a number on how old my soul is. As we discover what is true, we lift the veil to our soul-self and sharing consciousness. We remember who we truly are as a truth that is eternally so. Fear needs to be pulled back and replaced with trust. Risk a blind, unconditional leap of faith.

If we understand and integrate the reality of manifesting what we need, we can assume responsibility in our humanity. If I claim fear, I will manifest what I need to confront the source of fear so it can be released. That does not feel good, but it is a wonderful thing because if we are responsible, we will do the work necessary to release what is rancid. We, as our souls, benefit and will ascend in doing so. When we have completed lessons related to rancid experiences, we move into a higher frequency (which feels good) and now manifest what we need. We can step into tomorrow and not know what will be manifested on our behalf. We can trust in the truth, which will be for our ultimate benefit. It will not be what we as ego want, but rather what we need to ascend. They may overlap at times, and it is nice when what we want is what we need. The more aligned and conscious we become of our Divine Plan, the more that occurs naturally.

That is flow.

Ascendance as a soul is natural, and it's the purpose of our time here. Once we become conscious of it, our life shifts in purpose and meaning.

Service

As you go deeper on this journey, you will become aware of how service will be a source of personal meaning. You may realize that your own spiritual ascendance has a dramatic impact on others and that it may assist in elevating both humanity and the planet. This does not necessarily mean we need to change what we do for a living, though some may feel the need to do so. We are in service simply through being who we are.

The energetic expansion has an immediate impact on those around you on a soul level. It excites their souls to also want to ascend. That may mean making their lessons stronger, the rancid in their life more rancid tasting, and thus harder to ignore. It may seem like as you ascend, the people around you get worse. They do in one sense, but from a divine perspective, they are lovingly being gifted with pain as a teacher, pointing to the chapter in the book they need to focus on.

They are being called to ascend. What a different spin to put on what may appear to be a disaster!

The divinity of atrocity can be seen in action here, and you, in your higher frequency, may have triggered it! This is being in service. No need to feel shame. Compassion does not take responsibility away from that person but prompts and supports them in stepping in the direction they now need to move. You cannot do this for them; they must be the ones to take responsibility. We can support them by helping prepare and increasing readiness, rather than taking actual steps. If you pay attention, you will see their soul steps forward to prompt these shifts. When I take my trauma clients into higher frequency, after lifting the dense heaviness, their spouses or living partners often suddenly spiral downward, seemingly out of the blue. It's this process I just described.

We may also see people be inspired by the shift in us, and if they have no need to experience rancid, they will instead move in the direction of becoming aware and seek such answers and deeper meaning. It all depends on what people need, but we become the catalyst whether we recognize it or not. Appearances can be deceiving. We are all born with the capacity to fully ascend and self-realize. This may not have been in our contracted Divine Plan, but that is not written in stone. We are always encouraged and supported to move beyond that plan if it is in the direction of ascension. An extraordinary exception is currently being made to allow people to skip multiple journeys as human incarnates to ascend.

Energy self-directs and will flow first to where you need it. You can also use your mind to direct energy to a particular place or to someone else, but intention is key. Another heart-centered approach is sawing your breath through your heart chakra. As you breathe, imagine one of those old two-man blade saws, like in the old *Popeye* cartoons. Imagine your breath as that long saw, sawing through your heart center as you breathe in and out. This too will open your heart center. This, however, can simply be used as a gentle reminder to shift into being in your body instead of being upstairs. We can use this all the time. We can still think and be in relationships, it just changes where we find our center of being. Being heart-centered creates a shift and opens us up to receiving intuitively. It allows us to practice mindfulness with less effort and provides an opportunity to detach from our ego addiction. It is gentle in that I am still who I am, but from a different perspective. Being in service also moves us away from ego-centricity, as being in service involves others besides us. Energetically, we want to hold the intention of being in service with everything we do, every action we take. Everything we do indirectly supports this effort. The energy of service shifts our frequency of being within this dimension.

Frequency and Dimension

As we scroll through the dial on a radio, we may stop at a particular station, a particular frequency to tune into. We may hear music. If we go a little further and stop at another point on the dial, we hear a news report. If we keep going to another frequency on the dial, we may tune into a station announcing a sports event. The stations live in specific frequencies along a spectrum of radio waves. As we tune in to a station, we can hear the sports event, music, or news. The sports event has not ended if I am tuned into music. Likewise, the news is still being reported. This is analogous to frequencies that we experience in our current place on the dial.

We are electric. We process emotions as energy. We carry a current and operate at a particular frequency unique to us. I have discussed raising that frequency to access information that is available only when we tune into that station. Emotions each vibrate at different frequencies. Fear and shame vibrate as slow, lower vibrations, while joy and love are very high frequency emotions. If we raise our frequency high enough, fear and shame cannot manifest. Thus, working to self-realize, we need to release those parts of us still holding onto shame and fear. We cannot bring shame and fear into the next station. If we raise our frequency, we experience this dimension differently. Just as the news is still being broadcast while I tune into music, I simply do not experience it. I do not experience the fear-laden events of my past when tuned into a higher frequency. I do not need to, as this served me at one time, but not now. I can honor it, as it helped me get here. I do not hold it in regret or with remorse. I hold it in honor, as from it I learned, let go, and moved on. I do this regardless of whether it was fear, grief, shame, regret, or something else. I still hold it in honor.

We are tuned into the third dimension (3D) of twelve dimensions. There are thirty-three dimensions, and models with more than twelve exist, but I will use twelve to teach with. Picture a big radio dial. We are tuned into station three of twelve presets. When someone dies and crosses over into another dimension, we think they have risen to Heaven, somewhere far away, beyond the clouds. However, they are right here with us, simply existing at a different frequency. That is why, if someone is grieving, I can help them connect to their deceased more easily than I can connect. Their loved ones sit right in the room with us, right next to the person related, only at the next frequency on the dial. The grieving person is very tuned into the energy of the person who passed; thus, they are energetically closer to them.

We simultaneously exist in different dimensions, even bilocating at times! Consciously bilocating at will is possible at some point, as I can do this now. It is energetically being at two places dimensionally at the same time. I can also bilocate within this dimension. Each dimension serves a very particular function. We do not consciously recognize this, as we are focused on the dimension we are tuned into, but what happens here affects the aspect of us in higher dimensions. We are multidimensional beings, but rarely have we had that experience or understanding. When we live in lower frequencies, engaging challenges (lessons), we are mired in our third dimensional reality. When we can lift and begin to integrate ideas of our soul, we vibrate at a higher version of 3D. When we are unveiled and open intuitively to consciously align with our Divine Plan, then we taste the fourth and fifth dimensions. We tune in between stations and receive the reception of both. We were always multidimensional, only now, we experience this consciously. People who channel spirit simply tune into a higher frequency while still living in 3D.

This book is being written as a multidimensional experience. The concepts are from a higher frequency, but I have taken on the challenge to present these ideas so they can be understood from a lower-frequency experience.

In soul realization, we are conscious of being multidimensional. Note that the actual dimensions being linear are presented that way for learning and understanding. In higher consciousness, such linear scales do not really exist as such and are realized differently.

Please note that the energies we work with, aside from the vibrational ones we can manage, are also affected by energies coming up from the Earth as well as energies coming down from the cosmos. These energies change daily (every twelve hours), and thus the summary experience of being who we are changes daily. We have good days and rough ones. Some days we feel great, but it does not sustain at that level because all these other energies change daily. We are never in one state, energetically. There are also other influences, such as lunar cycles, astrological shifts and cycles, sun cycles, eclipses, equinoxes, and solstice events. Calendar dates, such as certain holidays and numeric sequences, can also create portals or vortices that allow us to access more energy than usual. This sounds complicated, but just consider it and perhaps use this to understand why we feel low energetically one day and then feel great the day after. It may be just the blend of frequencies in combination with what we are doing energetically at the time.

At times, when portals open and they hit with us a greater share of cosmic energy, we may be affected in several ways. At a lower frequency, we may not notice. If we are working through stuff and doing release work, that experience will temporarily intensify, or we will become aware of new release targets. This is because the light coming in seeks space and forces the darkness within us to be dislodged. We may feel worse, but do not be fooled. The bad feeling serves a good purpose, as you become aware of that which you need to be responsible for to evolve. Those doing release work will feel lifted to a new level via a tweak in frequency! As we adapt to these new, higher frequencies, we need to pay attention to self-care. Our body may feel sick or sluggish. It will pass, but we need to listen and respect the need to rest or retreat from pressure for a day until it passes.

Deepening our awareness to nuanced micro shifts will help us be aware of energies and their infinite combinations, influencing our experience of being. It will pull us from egoic experience as such, via awareness, to very subtle sensations. Feeling energy will help you connect to your soul, as your soul is energy. Eventually you will understand energy as a language. It holds nonlinear knowing type information. It is beyond what we understand as thought, as thought is linear in design. Thought follows the inherent unspoken rules about what we understand to be real and makes logical sense of such.

I can knock on this hard, wooden desk and know the thought experience of its solid feel—it is real. It is finite and has fixed boundaries. What I see and feel sensorially influences my ideas defining the linear experience of the desk. However, if I raise my frequency to a higher location on the dial, I can see the desk in its pure energetic form. It is dayglow green, and this glowing, cloudlike, almost formless form dances before me, moving rapidly and changing constantly. That is quite different when I tune back into 3D. There is an applicable Buddhist koan: "Things are not as they seem, nor are they otherwise." This is not a linear idea!

When I would shoot infrared film of nature in early spring—when plants emit the strongest amount of infrared radiation—I could not see through the almost black filter and had to guess exposures. I developed and printed my own photography at the time, and it shocked me to see these twenty to thirty-foot-high cloudlike ghosts swirling about on the path I walked! The naked eye could not see them. Instead, they could only be captured on infrared-treated film with special filtration. It was seeing beyond our own visual spectrum. When you walk into a room and suddenly feel the anger or depression of an individual in that room, you taste that person energetically. It is beyond linear thought that you know that person is going through something intense. After all, you have not talked to them but have this sense to stay away or not interact. That sense is nonlinear. It does not follow the logical sequence of knowing by deductive reasoning. It is information known through the energetic expression of emotion.

Most energy and subtle energy expressions are beyond the requirements of logic and reason. For example, the desk, experienced in its energetic form, is not experienced as an idea or experience that is not true. It is experienced as indisputably real, just as the 3D version. Our experience of being expands when we consider both linear and nonlinear experience. Focusing on subtle energy expands us by introducing new ways to obtain information. It may be information beyond words or language. It may be language-based, such as this book, as evidence as such. Accept that possibility, and just know. This is another level of trust. It is trusting that subtle experiences of energy will inform us in some way. It is trusting the unknown. Experiencing ourselves via such subtle energy is experiencing our soul within our field.

PART IV

PREPARING FOR SOUL CONNECTION

Chapter 5

SOUL LENS

We have now learned to "see" through two different lenses—ego and awareness. An expansion occurs when we move from ego to awareness, and now, we will expand further as we step into an awareness of being conscious, or conscious awareness. Conscious awareness is pulling way back and seeing the big picture. If awareness is a wide-angle view, conscious awareness is an ultra-wide view. From this ultra-wide angle, we have the advantage of taking in what is happening and perhaps being able to see the context or meaning of why this may be happening now. Ego has us up close and center, but we are too close to have access to the meaning we can get from pulling back. Practicing seeing through this lens helps us practice for seeing through the soul lens.

The influence of soul creates the difference between seeing through conscious awareness and the soul lens. The energy of soul (once you can get this to be steady) is a higher frequency and prevents us from experiencing shame or fear. That influences our decision-making and allows us to take positive risks without interference from ego. Our soul's energy field is a consciousness that eventually merges with ours. This is merging with your Higher Self, and that influences how you perceive information and how you react. I notice people who are practiced working with soul lens say when presented with problems or challenges, they see solutions. The difference they are experiencing is they receive information via knowing rather than thinking. Thinking with language is a function of our brain. Knowing is a nonlinear language we realize; it is not thought-dependent. For example, I know you will be challenged by this idea, as you are not connected to your soul yet, which will provide evidence. I did not have to think that idea, as it is a truth, like the sky is blue.

Intro to Soul

Before I walk you through the process of connecting to your soul, let's take a closer look at what it involves. You can refer to this writing as needed once you connect and practice being one with your soul. In the meantime, practice the Flow exercise and ask your Higher Self to *Flow* high frequencies to raise your vibration. Notice the feeling of tingly energy in your field. That is energy from your soul! Use this as a reference point and repeat as necessary throughout the journey.

In the awareness of the energetic presence of our soul, we expand.

Our soul's energy consists of love, but as frequency, it feels more like energy. This will shift as we evolve. It is a co-conscious state of being. We need our body to hold this energy for our soul to stick around. It takes time to maintain that as a steady state, but we can play around when we do. We ask our soul to increase the frequency and intensity. We acclimate to that in a week or so and again ask to bump it up again. The cycle will go on autopilot, and a new journey begins. This version of love in its expanding form is complex to describe, as it operates at a much higher frequency than the emotional love we are used to, and it is experienced as much as energy as emotion.

Physically, we feel energy moving around us in all directions. Our crown and heart feel open. If we get used to flowing this energy in our field, we will be in conscious awareness and see and experience the world through this lens. It will be the same *and* different.

As loving energy flows outward, we will project this, and the universe will reflect love back to us. It will change your experience of the world, and you will notice people around you respond differently as they too, consciously or unconsciously, experience your shift. Your values will change, past issues of importance may seem minor now, and what becomes a priority may be more influenced by the love that you embody. Attachment to material things may lessen, as we now realize they have less or a different value.

Our perception shifts, and we begin to be more aware of what is true, what feels right—regardless of written rules that may say otherwise. We can feel what is true, not just what is considered morally right or wrong. Truth is beyond cultural morality. This does not mean we will be immoral by all cultural standards, as most of our morality systems base themselves on the common sense of what is true. However, some local, cultural distortions of morality exist and do not hold up as truth in some cases.

I have mentioned prior how, in some religions or parts of the country, a strong, culture-based paternalism (male-dominated) often discriminates against women and other groups, viewing them as separate or unequal. This may be unforgiving and judgmental, even viewing these groups as sinners who can never be forgiven or included in their religious order. Some evangelical organizations have cited moral issues as code for gender and racial discrimination. In truth, we are one—One with All. In our past lives, we likely have lived as both male and female and gay or nonbinary at different times. We may have been different races, ethnicities, and from different financial classes. Our soul holds all these experiences within itself. Our soul has a memory of all its existences, and for us to think that this incarnation defines who we are is a mistake. We are so much greater.

We may be restricted from knowing too much, as we would be overwhelmed and would not be able to handle it all. Our soul will gift us with what we need to know based on our readiness to know such. I found that over time, knowing has replaced thinking, as my merger with soul consciousness is complete. We just need to be lovingly open and receptive. We may investigate our human heritage via genealogy, but our soul has its own genealogy, which has little to do with family lineage. Ironically, we are more defined by our soul's past lives than our family ancestry. We just start to see beyond structures or regulations as limitations as we peek over the wall and see what is possible. We see conflict and, at the same time, see resolution.

Our Aura

Normally, we sense that we end where our skin ends, but energetically, we extend about two to three feet in every direction—the average length of our auric field. This allows us to taste the surrounding energy much like an insect uses antennae. We may sense if someone in the room feels angry or depressed as soon as we walk in. We get that information by tasting their energy with our aura, sampling their auric field. You can sense your aura by putting your palms up, facing outward, but close to your body. Start to *slowly* move your hands away from you, stopping when you sense what feels like a wall of air or subtle wind. If you trace this subtle boundary up, around, and down below you, you will see this bubble surrounds you 360 degrees.

People who have had traumatic experiences as children may have learned to automatically expand their auric field to detect oncoming danger. As adults, they may have an aura that extends too far out, and as a result, they feel everyone else. They live as unwilling empaths. If we imagine shrinking this field to be only two to three feet from our skin, we will not feel others as strongly.

If you are an empath, pulling back is not automatic. If you go out shopping and do not want to feel everyone else, you must manually call your aura back each time. If done over and over, however, you may condition your aura to not expand when you go out. If you ask your aura to come in closer, it will listen to you and respond as you intend. It is a part of you—a protector. In our childhood, this part of our energy system acts to protect us. Then, when we get older, it takes protection orders from our now-developed ego. If it learned to expand in fear, this conditioned response will not change unless you condition a new, different response.

Expanding Our Experience of Being

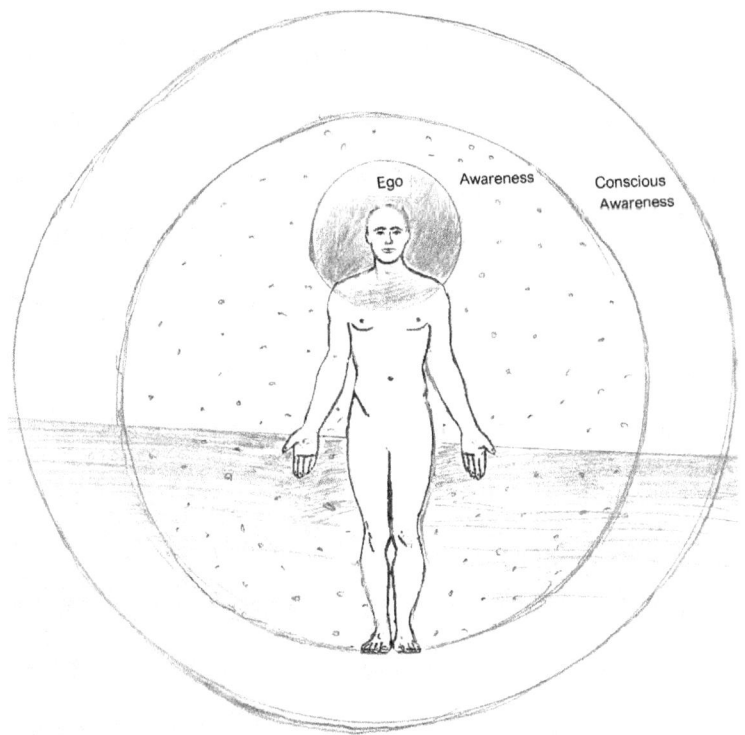

When our energy expands as we realize our existence as love, it has nothing to do with our aura. The energy moving outward can be felt, but this does not relate to our aura's status. Being one with nature is an expansive idea. We're one with the sky and stars above us, and that takes us beyond our skin. Add loving energy to that expansion, and the energy powers up. The more open and expansive we are, the more love we are open to experience, the higher our frequency will ascend.

There seems to be no limit to how high we can ascend energetically, except the limitation created by what we can physically handle and what we are ready to realize. Energy comes packed with information. It is another way of *knowing* without thought. The concepts that are presented in higher consciousness are difficult for our minds to wrap around. The idea that we manifest our world is difficult to digest in a lower frequency but becomes obvious at a higher frequency.

Another example is that no linear time exists in higher dimensions. The past, present, and future all present at once. They simultaneously impact each other in the present. *All time* feels too big to fit in our small heads (thus it is experienced via conscious awareness). It is a concept brought in with high frequency. In a way, this is another level of expansion. If we exist as a soul and start to realize this energy, we must prepare to handle that high frequency. We do this by experiencing samples and acclimating to that level. We will then be bumped up incrementally over time to be able to handle such. As energy, we expand with realization of higher, more expansive frequencies. No instructions inform us on expanding; it happens automatically. It moves us closer to whom we are as Source energy, and it becomes easy to be in oneness with God, regardless of any previous belief or lack thereof.

The concept of immortality is also expansive. Our soul moves from lifetime to lifetime in a cycle of evolution-based continuance. We evolve with each new journey, be it a human one or otherwise. Our deceased loved ones stay close by and never really die in a sense. Our relationship with them as a physical being has ended, and that must be grieved. However, they are not in that body six feet under or in the ashes in the urn upon the fireplace mantle. They live as spirit, one dimension up. We inhabit what is referred to as the third dimension, as all is 3D (form-based). Our deceased loved ones inhabit the Astral Plane. As I described earlier, it is possible to access our loved ones and honor their continuance. This busts us out of this box we have placed ourselves in, that our lives are finite. From a more expansive view: Life is temporary, and we continue, but in another form. Infinite is without limitation. If we regard ourselves as infinite and eternal as a truth, we expand.

We continue infinitely.

INTUITION

The language of the soul is something you already know but perhaps need to start listening to. We can "know something" and have a strong gut feeling. We may feel a shift in energy or temperature. Suddenly, we get a chill or become excessively warm or even briefly nauseous. We experience most of our intuitive information in our chest. Our heart chakra is said to be the matrix of the soul.

When intuitive information manifests, I can sometimes trace the flow from crown to heart, but I mostly just receive through my chest area. To be open to intuitive guidance, which can be guidance from your soul, spirit team, or other celestial advisers, we develop a mindful awareness of our heart center. If we become heart-centered, we will be more open to receive. If we center in our head, we will think and trigger ego. This experience closes us off to openness and will provide the distrust and doubt to discount any hits we may notice. Intuitive guidance, however, is sacred, as it may be God speaking through you. It always prompts us to do what is in our highest interest. Our souls, spirit teams, and advisers all have a bigger picture of our life. They know where we are headed and can therefore prompt us to learn or act in an ultimately beneficial way. Sometimes the information is loud, not in an audible way, but in knowing.

If you are clairaudient, you may hear information. I receive more in the way of energy that seems to provide information, but at times it seems like I hear and see it. It is strange and hard to describe. As you become more heart-centered, you will be less egoic. That means you will be more in the lens of awareness, so you can notice when switching to ego. You can always switch back by noticing things sensorial. Notice what you see, hear, taste, smell, and feel now. Challenge yourself to be concerned with only what happens now, in this very moment, and not a second beyond or prior. Bring yourself back to your heart. Resistance to leaving the head goes back to the ego feeling threatened. After some tug-of-war between head and heart, you will learn to feel at home at your heart center. Knowing this sensation can be subtle and easy to miss. When you start to tune in, to find subtle hints of knowing, you begin to realize how much you can be informed in this manner. Developing such awareness is a skill that takes practice and a quiet mind.

We will eventually find it easier to discern intuitive information from our thoughts. When we're body-centered, our mind is more likely to be quiet than when the head dominates. We just learned to view the world from another lens.

Three Lenses

There are three lenses through which we can experience being human.

One lens is ego, and if we know of this lens only, we make ourselves vulnerable to suffering and not finding true meaning in life. No one is exclusively egoic; it's just that they do not realize they switch between ego and the awareness lens (the second lens) hundreds of times a day.

We use awareness to drive our cars and find our way around. We taste food and smell with awareness. We feel our heart beating and hear someone calling our name. Awareness can be an exclusive lens to look through, though this takes practice and conditioning. Awareness can help us use ego and triggered feeling states to understand and explore challenges as lessons.

The third lens is that of our soul, known as *conscious awareness*. In the previous paragraphs, we discussed different ways we may experience being in the world and receiving information. Using intuition and energy combined with a pulled-back view is the lens of our soul. From our soul's lens, we can see the big picture and eventually derive meaning. When our soul is driving, we are co-creating reality. It is not in the context of "I." From an egoic lens, "Egoic-I" is driving. From an awareness lens, I am aware that I think *I am driving*. From a soul lens, there is no "I." There is the energy of being and becoming, and the I is experienced as all that is before me, as a manifestation I created. It is a lens through which we expand. We expand energetically in how we see our role in the world. It is a completely different picture than we get from the egoic lens. It is like taking pictures with infrared film. From an ego, we cannot experience what we experience as soul. It simply does not exist, and some of this writing may not be able to make sense to readers not there…yet.

Be patient. You will get this once you connect to your soul.

An Example of Three Lenses

If I receive a call from my doctor who tells me I have cancer, the Egoic-I immediately wants to resist. This is bad news, and I would rather deny it than accept it. I volunteer for more tests, as there must be some mistake. After several second opinions, I concede that I have cancer; I must accept the unacceptable. After allowing the fear to run out of gas, in awareness, I strategize with the medical team on how best to proceed. I weigh the options presented. Now, I have time to go deeper. I ask my soul, *Why am I manifesting cancer currently? What purpose does this serve? What lesson is cancer prompting me to learn?*

With hypnotherapy, we can ask the cancer. It reveals the issue of lack of self-love. It's about the unworthiness I never paid attention to. I go deeper and find the source in my early childhood. I realize I am worthy and always have been. I can love myself and even experience myself as love. The cancer has served its purpose of calling attention to this. Now, I can let it go and heal with treatment, and unless my life plan includes an early check-out, the cancer will (or may) remit. This is a demonstration of three lenses.

The initial fear and resistance demonstrate the reaction of ego, which only sees this as a hopeless and fatal situation. Awareness, a more emotionally neutral view, allows acceptance to join with medical advisers on a plan. Here, I am emotionless as I take in information about odds and what the treatments will entail. I simply let reality in. I am not happy about it, but I do not resist or deny it either. In this space, I can explore what my soul wants to show me (soul lens). I get someone to help me go deep and deeper still until I realize a truth. Our soul directs us away from what is not true by manifesting pain, rancid taste, and, yes, even cancer (personal atrocity).

Our soul is of God or Source, and discovering truth reveals this. The divinity of looking at a traumatic atrocity through a lens that brings us closer to truth unmasks experiences that serve a higher purpose or knowing. Claiming reality through this soul lens is claiming our own divinity as one with all. We manifest the atrocity to learn what we need as a soul. We may collude with others to jointly manifest such greater lessons. This can only be understood through the lens of our soul. Everything has purpose and meaning. We do not arbitrarily manifest things to experience. We manifest what is most beneficial to us and what may be a benefit indirectly or directly to others. The work of our soul always serves the big multidimensional picture, as we do not exist in a vacuum. We impact others as they impact us, as our environment impacts us, expanding or contracting as necessary. As we realize our Divine Plan through the lens of awareness or conscious awareness (our soul), we experience expansion, especially when coming from the egoic lens. Next, let's dive deeper into this idea of contraction or expansion, both internally and through the world.

Expansion and Contraction

Here is a simple visualization you can incorporate into your meditation practice.

Imagine bringing the sun or a star into the center of your chest. Feel it there as an ever-expanding, brilliant ball of light. Feel its heat. Merge with it as it expands outward. You may bring love in as well, to expand with the light radiating outward. Be the experience of expanding. Stay with it until just the experience of expanding as you remains. In other words, let yourself become the sun within you. Feel the radiating waves of light permeate every molecule of your being. Imagine the energy that you radiate as healing and allow whatever parts of you needs healing to be washed with these healing rays.

Stay with this if you can (twenty minutes, if possible) to allow healing to complete. In joining the idea as expansion, we raise our frequency. You share this experience with your soul.

Coming out of that meditation, notice the shift in view, in energy, and perception of self. Use awareness to notice what happens as we attempt to resize our experience of being to fit in our body again. Now, our view is different (contraction). I am not a star or the sun. I am not expanding; I can access I, or me, if I choose. My boundaries take the same shape as before I lost them. This is switching from a soul lens to an awareness lens.

Now let's bring in a memory of what you just experienced. Remember this expanded state and how the energy felt. Hold this memory, and you may feel the energy and even re-experience some expansion. This demonstrates a dual awareness now, being aware of two dimensions of frequency. If you imagined a sun in your chest, your imagination opens to new possibilities. The conscious brain does not know the difference, in meditation, between imagined and non-imagined reality. Our consciousness believes the sun swells in our chest, so we feel the energy and expand. This experience can raise you into the fourth dimension as you relax into the energies. As you remember and partly re-experience, you are multidimensional. You already are a multidimensional being, but here we play with becoming aware of different conscious states.

If, during the meditation, you became frightened of losing control and pulled out, you then switched to ego state, as fear will always provide an egoic lens. If that happened, try it again, but for brief periods of time, to learn that letting go will not endanger you. Start with five minutes and then ten. Be gentle, and do not judge. It gives you permission to do something different.

Can you bring in this memory of higher frequency as a feeling state to your day-to-day operations and interactions with others? It takes a little practice, and repeating the meditation daily helps. Experience the energy as a knowing. This practice holds a higher frequency of consciousness. You will find that the higher frequency changes your view and decisions. Experiment and notice the shifts.

The experience of expanding and contracting is familiar to us and our soul, as we contract and expand throughout our lifetime. Breathing is the act of expanding and contracting. Our heart beats through this action. The universe expands and contracts. We contract and expand to be birthed. Moving from trauma and pain to bliss is contraction and expansion. Moving from duality (separateness) to oneness is an expansion from contraction, even though we are going from two to one. The undulating energies of Earth and Cosmos dance together in a spiral of contraction and expansion with ongoing change.

We can see expanded and contracted states expressed in people's postures. A depressed person has her head down, body caved in, curled in a protective ball. Someone who just crossed the finish line of a marathon feels like they can do anything. Their crossing posture spreads wide open, arms expanding high in the air, announcing their victory.

Can you look or listen to someone and notice if they are expanding or contracting? Can you check in with yourself during the day and notice whether you are in expansion or contraction? If we are contracting, can we change that? Recognize that lessons act as expansions and contractions of consciousness.

Our communal sense of morality—what society agrees upon to be right or wrong, good or bad—may not align with the concept of lessons or why lessons manifest. For example, it may feel bad that I got fired, but lesson-wise, it may be the best thing ever, as now I am free to take on take on a new, better-suited position. We may do something that we regret, like inflicting pain on someone, though we never intended to hurt them. They may separate from the relationship as a result, opening the way for better, more meaningful relations down the road for both individuals. We did not realize that we were supposed to do this; it is not messing up, in hindsight. It may have been a strained relationship that we just did not have the strength to break off from. So, an accident manifests to help us along.

There are no accidents! It would be difficult to bring a righteous model to this, seeing it as black and white, wrong or right. In lessons, that does not always apply as we hold the big picture. Two souls may have contracted to help each other evolve, and this may require one to harm or murder the other. On Earth, in this 3D plane of consciousness, this is immoral and wrong. But, on a soul plane, if we understood it was agreed upon to achieve a higher purpose, perhaps we would refrain from judgment. The apparent contraction was part of a latent expansion!

A perfect example is when George Floyd was killed at the hands of several police while a bystander took a cell phone video that went viral, kicking off an anti-racism movement worldwide. Obviously, America and the world had a lesson regarding racist policing practices to learn. Perhaps the souls of George Floyd and the police contracted to do this in afterlife, agreeing to meet at that corner and included was the cellphone videographer, who, oddly, was never told to put her phone down. A contraction that expanded worldwide!

Our lessons and evolution may often involve others. We cannot use our thinking mind to make sense of such complicated manifestations, and, at times, we just need to acknowledge there is a reason for everything. We just may not be privy to every reason.

An Extreme Example of Contraction and Expansion

In the past life regression where I survived Hiroshima, in afterlife, I was presented with a transition into oneness. Within an hour of our time, I went from a highly contracted state (horrific pain and suffering) to an extremely expanded state of divine realization and bliss. I could feel the contraction occurring as I realized being this person. Likewise, I could feel the expansion several times in afterlife, but especially in the last part I witnessed. I had to stop it, as the expansion became too much. I did not shut down the pain as being too much, even though it was. I shut down the ascending bliss as it continued to ascend, and I was at a point where I just could not handle any more of the higher frequency. What I describe here is an extreme example of expansion from contraction, and, of course, when I bought out of that experience, I contracted some again. I present this extreme as a claim for what is possible. I will try describing the expansion I experienced, as it may plant seeds for those reading this.

First, the energy calmed me, as I was agitated—but it also felt healing, as any vestige of pain from remembering my human experience lifted. It was not like being drugged; it was more like the emotional components dissolved or evaporated. It felt good, and I was able to then relax and permit deepening to happen. It was healing, like my entire life of pain and suffering was smoothed over. It just lifted from me as though it never happened, yet I never gave up knowing who I was or where I had just come from. That would be used as a background context of the higher energies. I always was co-conscious that I survived an atrocity, but that knowing did not have a deep, painful charge. It simply provided context, a reference point. With that awareness in the background, I felt the energy increasing in frequency. I was gradually lifted into a higher state and became curious. I am not sure if this was my Hiroshima-self or my present self-witnessing this that became curious, but I recall getting up from reclining and looking around.

There was pipeline connected to the room (hanging off the top of the wall—no ceiling) that ran off into the distance and out of sight. Then, the information began to flow with the energy. As I looked to see the source of this pipe, a knowing came over me. I knew the source was God. I had no concept of God as a human, yet in knowing, the irrefutable truth became clear instantly. At once, it shifted me, and my whole being felt this. It was another level, and I wish I could describe what that felt like. I was flooded with knowing. Like a faucet opened and information flowed. I learned that what happened was supposed to happen and why. No mystery, all answers.

I stayed calm as I took this in. It made sense, and I integrated this knowing instantly as I learned it. The energy was now increasing and getting stronger. I was becoming one with God. It was a knowing that arose in the energetic realization. I felt one with all, expanding, now radiant and exceeding all boundaries. I attempted, as a witness, to stay with this as long as I could, but the intensity kept increasing and rapidly. It exceeded my physical human boundaries. The frequency became so high and so intense, it became intolerable. It did not seem that it would stop. I was not able to contain or sustain any more and opened my eyes to bring myself back to the present.

The 3D me rationalizes this as a just reward for what my Hiroshima lifetime had lived through. However, this rationalization happened in 3D, so such rationalizations cannot be applied. I have been privileged with knowing this lifetime followed this incarnation, and that I will not be returning as a human incarnate after this. I know I am a very old soul, and my journeys have included at least two lifetimes where divine realization occurred. Many theorize that once realization happens, we no longer cycle back into human form. Obviously, that isn't true, or there are exceptions. I can see that this Hiroshima life connects to the other lifetimes experienced through my regressions. I feel like my current lifetime is meant to be the dot connector for my soul's past—as the grand human finale. I am the final act, and perhaps I saw Hiroshima and met Anna Brown to take those lessons into my practice and then into a book so a larger audience can benefit (expansion).

My service was incomplete, so here I am! Knowing all this changes the meaning in my life as I shift in understanding of why I am here. Not everyone is where I am at in our soul's historic evolution. Until recently, I never had a clue any of this would happen to me. Apparently,

I was ready for what I have been shown, or I would not have had such experiences. You may be a younger soul, but do not be discouraged. I opened this book with a warning: Earth is approaching critical mass. We are endangered as a planet now—cataclysmically so. The point of no return is within reach, and it is on us to change course and be responsible. Humanity's choices and failure to learn have us repeating lessons that worsen as I write this. Earth is energetically contracting when it should be expanding.

Expansion and contraction qualify conscious awareness, calls attention to it, makes it more experiential—like giving it a texture. We add on to and play with this idea, and as we do, we slip into conscious awareness! What will follow are more concepts, more qualifiers that help us see differently so we can be practiced in this new state of consciousness. Sometimes these devices point to ego, attachments to ego, or to lessons present but not on our radar. We may be using time to reveal such attachments or lessons. View these as tools to apply to shifting our attachments, as they are different ways to look at the reality we deal with daily.

Timelines

A timeline is an experience attached to a particular range within linear time that we are all familiar with.

Linear time provides convenience, offering a scheduled structure to live and work within. Time is an essential part of this structure, broken into units called appointments. *We* create sub-timelines. If I am told I have a terminal illness with limited life expectancy, a new timeline is established. My world suddenly has shifted importance to this new timeline. For a lighter example—"Summer is coming, and I have only so much time to prepare to present in a bathing suit"—could be used. I have a timeline within the greater timeline we use for living. Other timelines may have been created by trauma.

Let us say I had a period as a kid where I worked hard to be "good enough." No matter how much I overachieved, I was never rewarded with validation or praise. I can see how this still impacts my current behavior, as I still strive to "overachieve" with no satisfying goal of my own. This is an attachment to an old timeline that no longer serves me. In fact, it holds me back from a more positive and pleasurable life. Letting go or collapsing old, unneeded timelines can be very freeing. Timelines point to lessons.

Can you be aware of timelines that may still impact you? How attached to them are you? What if we let go and changed our experience of time and being?

That general experience of being, of existing before any ideas or thoughts, is conscious awareness, or the experience of consciousness. It is the experience shared by our eternal soul. Can you just *be* and let go of the 3D linear timeline? Join your soul and *just be eternal for a moment*. Like trying on new clothing—how does eternity feel? It may not feel any different, or you may sense confusion as you step into the unknown. You are playing with truths about existence and the experience of different timelines. Within a moment, we may experience linear time, all time, or eternity.

Earlier I shared an experience of pre-experiencing time after doing Qigong exercises. It challenged the idea that I must make intellectual sense of every aspect of the world I live in. I was shown through *knowing* that this linear timeline is an illusion—one collectively accepted as a vast convenience. In her book, *The Field*, Lynne McTaggart said, "If consciousness is operating at the quantum frequency level, it also naturally resides outside space and time, which means theoretically we have access to information, 'past' and 'future.'"[7] I, thus, accidentally stumbled onto Lynne's quantum theory, clueless at the time. I experienced other times within this timeline when doing past life regressions. I was experiencing 1945 as a Hiroshima survivor, yet simultaneously experiencing the present. That happened because our soul holds *all*

---

7   Lynne McTaggart, The Field (New York: HarperCollins, 2008), 175.

time. The past, as I relived it, was informing the present. As my present is informed and changed, simultaneously my future is impacted and shifted. The past, future, and present were lived at once, though I may only have been conscious of the past and present. When I asked Anna Brown (the slave regression) what I needed to know, she knew exactly why I was there, as a witness to her lifetime, visiting from her future. We can only know of other timelines through *knowing*. All time is a truth known through realization but can be experienced via meditation and hypnotic experiences. It is a truth because it exists beyond time but not as something familiar in this 3D frequency. Yet we can experience all time as knowing alongside linear time.

We can now experiment with releasing unneeded timelines.

Not schedules or appointments that help us negotiate functioning, but rather those that we self-identify with. If we are emerging from trauma, we may attach to a timeline about where we have come from or what we have been through. We may hold that struggle up as a badge of honor. But we have moved on from that place and no longer need that badge to define us. I may say, "I have all this work experience—I should be earning higher pay." Here our idea of self-worth is tied to a timeline of work. While there may be validation in having worked a certain amount of time, we can be worth more pay because, in truth, we simply have the qualifications. We are deserving and worthy. This may be about unfinished lessons about self-worth, but we use the attachment to a timeline to point that out.

Sometimes such timelines are hidden or work in the background. We may limit ourselves or delay acting in a way that will advance us due to an irrational belief embedded in such a timeline.

"I am too old to go back to school or change careers."

"Because I haven't stuck with an exercise program in the past, I cannot try a new or different way to be fit."

As we grow and lose our *I* and *me*, these timelines pop into awareness via the *resistance* we experience them through. Suddenly, I am aware of a timeline as a limitation. We can explore and see if there is a lesson and release as necessary. Perhaps we can just notice and let it go. We may have many such timelines alive, holding us back from accessing our greatest version of who we are. They may be subtle and hidden. Becoming aware of them is a good place to start, and specialized therapies or energy work may be needed to dissolve or collapse these unwanted timelines if they seem stuck.

If you attend EMDR or a trauma therapy that processes meaning in memory, we have an "Ah-ha" moment. Imagine we processed memories that support the idea "I do not matter." A lifetime of evidence is released as a lie when we look back and see this was not about us. We disengage from the timelines holding the false contexts. We disengage the idea, and it loses its attachment to time, as knowing is consciousness and is outside of time. We realize the lesson "I matter, and I have *always* mattered." Take this new, but ancient, idea and make it eternal (as *always*). Can we move this knowing into all time, into the eternal state that truths live in? Truth is an eternal state free of timelines.

Conscious awareness of timelines helps us have another view of being present. We see the world and everyone in it with an awareness of seeing time differently. Now, we will develop another view of being to add to expansion, contraction, and timelines.

Contexts

We live in a world defined by context.

Contexts are labels we identify ourselves or others by. Each context is a mental construct created to provide a structure to understand the world. We think we need them. We can draw a parallel comparison to timelines. Timelines are an example of a context associated with a particular period. They only exist if we think. There are many contexts, and we can see they are optional. We may identify with being in a union. That is a context with which I self-identify. It may impact who I socialize with or who I vote for. I may identify as an alcoholic and have a defined community and a status within that community.

You can see how such a context can cause separateness and limitation. Contextual meaning, however, may be helpful. We give trauma recovery new meaning in this book by changing the label for a trauma to a lesson. This changes the context from suffering to a learning opportunity. Contexts are not good or bad but can be forms of unnecessary limitation. I point them out so we can use, ditch, or change them as needed. From the egoic lens, we do not believe we have any options. Contexts are the work of mind.

So, if I am separate from you but we are inseparably in a relationship via these words, it defies a collectively agreed-upon idea defining separateness based on form. The context of separateness insists that you and I end where our skin ends, yet you hold my most inner knowing in your hands. As you ingest these ideas as your own, that boundary becomes porous. I could easily prove I extend beyond my skin even by using scientific methods. It is simply an idea, and all contexts are ideas.

You and I, as energy, are an idea. We can manifest that experience and give it a sense of reality. We can identify that as context too. We imagine being love as a mental construct. Here, we use familiar pathways to realize truths that are beyond mind.

Consider eternity as an example. If I am to be eternal, I must first think of what eternity is. I need a sense of how long that is. It is too big to explain. It is like trying to contain love. We must therefore abandon thought and abandon time-related contexts to define eternity. Our surrender allows us to know what eternity is via another pathway. We *know* but not intellectually or with our mind. It is not possible to be eternal via mind. We experience love, change, expansion, energy, and eternity as conscious knowing. When we come back to the real world, we must bring our new experience of this reality as *re-known* through conscious awareness. While we live in conscious awareness, the rest of the world lives in a reality made of mental constructs. From our awareness, we can see the nature of these constructs—even those collectively created. They are just the nature of mind. This is why we feel detached. We are in higher consciousness as love energy. It does not require thought. The contexts that allow us to work and live are created by the mind. We can see that and still be in conscious awareness. We are not separate from such constructs but understand and experience them through a different lens.

There are two competing lenses: our ego lens (the land of neatly defined form, with boundaries) and soul lens (energy and movement that cannot be contained nor defined). The egoic lens is mind-derived, and the soul lens is consciously aware and soul-derived. We live consciously within a world complete with mind-manifested contexts and constructs. When you started this book, you had one, perhaps two, lenses. Now, we have taken a background awareness of being—consciousness—and played with making it into a primary experience. We still have an ego and an awareness lens. Only now we are learning to live in conscious awareness as a co-consciousness so we can still participate in the 3D world we live in. Perhaps one day we will be able to be in conscious awareness most of the time, if not exclusively. Perhaps one day the rest of the world will join us.

We have been investigating working from consciousness. In ego, we engage mind and thinking. Thus, egoic experience requires contexts. In awareness, thinking is optional, so context has less urgency. In the conscious awareness of our soul, context is not necessary. We can exist without context, though to work or engage 3D timelines, we can opt for contextual meaning. From a soul lens, if we identify with change and live free of a static idea of self, interdependent and one with the impermanence of all, that is free of context.

Imagine being in a spaceship hurdling through the universe at great speed. We look out the window and see the stars fly by. They provide context. Now imagine looking out to a space with no stars. Without that context, you cannot say how fast you are going or even if you are moving. If you stay with this, you will also realize that now, with no context, it does not matter. I no longer need to know if I am moving or not. The difference is we are not attached. I don't have to pick my social group, vote a certain way, or experience any artificial self-imposed limitation because of it.

Losing our attachment to even beneficial contexts can be freeing. It helps us be more open and flexible. I am limitless. This challenges not only our contexts but also our attachment to them. We move toward discovering who we are in truth.

Emptiness, Energy, Form

The Tibetan Buddhist phrase *Om Ah Hung* means "Emptiness, Energy, and Form."

Emptiness allows for the manifestation of all that is. Without emptiness, we could not exist, nor could anything. We, therefore, are inherently *emptiness*. I was emptiness before I existed, and now that emptiness exists inherently within my form. All form is inherently empty, manifested by energy into form. Stay with me as I try to clarify this abstract idea.

I think, therefore I am. The thought of who I am, manifested from emptiness.

Where else did it come from? The thought, as energy, and its form are inherently empty, or it could not manifest (and then unmanifest). It is the other side of the coin. This thought of *It will disappear* when I stop thinking it. Where will it go? It will unmanifest into its inherent empty state from which it began. If *I am* is a thought, emptiness, and form, then I can realize even my egoic idea of self is emptiness, manifested and unmanifested. It takes energy to manifest and unmanifest, illustrated by Om Ah Hung's words.

Energy is the catalyst between *form* and *emptiness*. We manifest at birth and unmanifest at death. Our soul changes its uniform. Everything around us manifests and un-manifests. We do this as we grow, evolve, and even conceive other humans, ideas, or creations. It is an unending dance of emptiness, energy, and form.

Our inherent empty nature exists so we can manifest. Likewise, we move through the process of self-realizing our inherent oneness that is a truth. Truth is an inherent, eternal state that is always manifested, but not always realized, like God.

An Experiential Exercise

Let us now revisit the concept of fear.

We know why fear exists. It is present to teach us, protect us, and to keep us safe. But let's step into that experience.

Give yourself permission to come with me as we re-examine it in a new way. Think of something that invites fear into your mind. Step into it like you would step into a garment. Feel it hacking your thoughts and asserting its dominance as it distorts our experience. It is doing what it is supposed to. It is difficult to trust in this energy. Notice how, from a calm state, we can manifest this uncomfortable feeling. Where did it come from? It came from the absence of fear as emptiness. So, what we are experiencing, as newly manifested, is inherently empty in nature. It has no physical form except that of energy. We saw in using tools like Pause and Flow that we can change energy rapidly. By tuning into another emotional station on the dial, fear changes like a chameleon.

Try letting fear go back to its empty state…

Fear does not cooperate that way! Its purpose is to stick around and ensure our wellbeing. It does not listen to any of our thoughts and will even shut down our ability to think. Be grateful that fear stays so tenacious. When we need fear, be assured it will manifest and present itself as dominant. Its temporary energy state manifests lovingly to protect us.

Imagine sending a grounding cable deep into the center of the Earth from your tailbone. Make it as wide as you need. Send the anxious energy down the cable. Use your imagination to prompt it along. Feel it drain from your face and head, from your hands and feet, and from everywhere else in your body. Scan and encourage any remnants of fear to follow its energy down this cable, safely into the center of the Earth. Scan again to check for any leftover fear.

Send it on its way.

Now manifest calm. Imagine your crown opening wide and a channel down your spine opening within you. Imagine a stream of light blue and violet calming energy and light flowing in and slowly making its way into your body, coating you internally with this wonderful calm, soothing energy. Go slow and give that energy time to manifest as Flow within you. Track it as it moves through your head and face, your internal organs and form, all the way to your feet and toes until you completely feel this energy.

You just manifested fear, unmanifested fear, and manifested calm.

Reality via Manifestation

With each breath we manifest the world before us in remarkable detail. If we step back, we realize this is stunning and miraculous. We are co-creators with God. We lovingly manifest what we need, lessons, and opportunities, or even inch toward knowing who we are authentically. We manifest every detail, what we dismiss as mundane as well as what we hold as important. We block manifestation and unmanifest as well. We also manifest what we experience in other dimensions and timelines. Allow your awareness to expand as you breathe and realize how large and expansive you are. Realize how sacred this vast and expansive understanding of being is.

We can manifest and unmanifest energies or emotions of being. Have you started to see how easy this can be? Imagine the world you live in. You manifested it, and it changes constantly. We have no idea what tomorrow will bring as our world shifts, always in a state of flux, manifesting, and un-manifesting. With that awareness and knowing, how solid is our world now? Our world is inherently empty, so it can potentially manifest. The energy frequencies are the necessary bricks and mortar to manifest form. Look around and notice the form appearances of objects in the room. A desk, a lamp, a chair, a pen, etc. Notice that they all appear solid but add the knowing that these objects hold an empty state within. Everything is energy and thus is mailable and can change. This idea is key to healing. It is key to manifesting or un-manifesting.

Our attachment to form will keep us anchored to suffering.

Our past circumstances were emptiness, turned into energy and form, purposed for us to experience, so they can be re-manifested (as lessons) but with a higher frequency. In hindsight, I can see the purpose of why I went through this, but now I see this differently. I claim my new reality as a higher frequency—it does not feel bad.

Form is inherently empty regardless of its deceptive solid appearance. I used energy and intention to unmanifest a bone spur coming out of my shoulder, and after six months, it vanished without a trace. I did not see it as a solid bone but as something inherently empty. It, as solid bone, un-manifested. I manifested it back to its original empty state, which I asked it to do via intention. Energy listens to intention and acted as the catalyst. Everything is energy.

Understand that our life shifts and flows. Let go and flow with the dance of this shifting energy and form as it manifests and un-manifests as necessary. Buddhists refer to this theory as impermanence. Everything changes, including us.

Nothing is permanent except change.

LIMITATION

Limitation starts as a thought, then energetically manifests.

It can take different forms. For example: a physical disability, a disease, a job, scarcity, loneliness, or perhaps discrimination. We may experience a glass ceiling in our workplace or feel stuck in a relationship. We may be locked in a prison—either literally or metaphorically. We may hold limiting beliefs about ourselves or what we can accomplish. Limitation is the suffering side of the coin.

If you are smart, you can intellectually manipulate an argument to justify any possible situation as a limiting factor. Just as Egoic-I feels real but only exists in thought, limitation is a point of view within the structure of our experience. We can learn from this rancid taste and go beneath the sense of lacking to discover its source. We can transcend any situation, knowing we experience limitation for a reason.

Let's say I am blind. That is a big limitation. I can either give up or move beyond such and live my life without compromise. Though I must adapt to a visual world with all my necessary accommodations, I, as a person, need not experience limitation. I can be limitless in my experience of love and flow in my Divine Plan.

Stephen Hawking suffered severe physical limitation but chose to experience limitlessness via physics and exploration into the vastness of the universe. In outer space, he no longer required a wheelchair or assistance. He no longer needed to see his body or disease as a limitation.

My past life as a slave was an extreme example of limitation, just as I was struggling with scarcity in my current life. For Anna Brown to show me how she transcended such a severe and painful extreme, immediately enabled me to see that my scarcity experience was not necessary and was sourced in feeling undeserving. I could then unmask this lie and release it. My financial situation stayed the same, but my point of view shifted. Energetically, I no longer supported the idea of not deserving abundance. My fortune did eventually change, but it changed faster when my frequency lifted as I embraced the idea of being limitless in every possible capacity. Everyone, even those experiencing the most impossible of limitations, can implement this necessary reframe.

You may feel resistance to the concept that we manifest our lives or the things that happen to us—both good and bad. Pull back and look at this as an idea rather than something literal. If I look at my situation as negative or stuck, does my negative attitude contribute to the problem? Is that something I can change and not engage in? This paradigm shift gives me control, as I now take charge of how I present my attitude and how I engage others. I may see that this is not about me. We investigate rancid, explore what can be different, and take steps toward change.

Conscious vs. Unconscious Manifestation

How do we create our world or influence the creation that we experience?

There are several factors that influence this, but it mostly comes down to energy. The collective manifests our immediate experience. The buildings, sky, trees, etc., are taken care of for us. We work in conjunction with collective manifestation, and sometimes we work against it.

Manifestation of our reality can be negative or positive in nature, depending on what we need to experience. Obviously, if we could choose, we would not want to experience trauma or difficult or painful challenges, even if we knew they harbor lessons for our ultimate benefit. Thus, we are shielded from such knowing. As an ill child, I recall having to swallow bad-tasting medicine. Our traumatic challenges are like that. We do not have to like them or want them. These bigger life lessons are prescribed to be learned before we take on our human incarnation. In the afterlife, we work with "Elders"—teams of experienced souls who have ascended and lived many lifetimes. They work with our soul in deciding what we experience in this next journey. This depends on our prior lives and goals. Those big challenges were unconsciously manifested before we were born.

We have an idea by now that if I don't learn a lesson, I will relive that lesson over and over until I get it. We energetically attract what we need, including players to participate in the lesson. Thus, we are responsible for manifesting, but also in manifesting the opposite.

I finally release my lesson on scarcity and can now manifest abundance.

We can be aware or made aware that we do this, so we call this conscious manifestation. We continue to participate in conscious manifestation but can also block or unblock manifestation. This may reframe the manifestation of scarcity. Using language differently sometimes is necessary or works better. We also can unmanifest as I did with my bone spur in my shoulder. That was also intended as asking the bone spur (form) to manifest back to its *empty* state. Everything is energy expressed as form or emptiness, so we can see this malleability in what presents as our reality.

Let us look at some evidence to support this theory. At the time of writing, I have been in private practice for eleven years. I treat trauma and have noticed that each person comes in with a particular flavor of trauma that repeated over and over in childhood and repeated multiple times in adulthood. These flavors included abandonment, physical abuse, sexual abuse, neglect, betrayal, loss, or being suffocated with care. Nobody presented with some of this and some of that. The betrayal victims stay true to form and only present betrayal trauma. Abandonment people do not mix it up with other types of traumas, as their lesson is regarding abandonment and not betrayal or something else. From a pulled-back view, this is remarkable evidence that each manifested their lesson as form particular to what they each needed.

Now, let's talk about unconscious manifestation.

Obviously, an unconscious action lies outside of our awareness. However, someone still does the manifesting. We can start big. The collective manifests the sky, trees, birds, sidewalk—everything we see when we walk outside. This kind of manifestation does not lie within our awareness, so we call it unconscious manifestation. Still, unconscious manifestation may be part of the lessons we need to experience.

One day, I was walking through a deli parking lot to get an iced coffee when a white SUV came plowing into me. Just as the vehicle made contact, I felt a vacuum over my head—a very strong pulling. I looked up, and up I went. I went up in the air feet first and back flipped safely, landing out of the way, softly on my belly. My head never hit the ground. Did I manifest any of that? I believe everything happens for a reason, so I get why this happened. My spiritual journey was about to launch to a new level, only I was not aware of it until that moment. I was not planning on getting hit by a car or being saved from getting hit. So, this was unconscious manifestation. Getting hit was a soul-contracted event. It had to happen. Thus, this was unconsciously manifested by my soul. My soul was consciously manifesting the event, though that was not conscious to me, thus an unconscious manifestation.

When we complete the big lessons, we can work with our soul on ascension and our Divine Purpose. We can now play with and explore what we want to do and move in the direction that feels good. This may or may not mean a change in job, relationship, or residence. It may just mean we choose to take on a new or old hobby. As we align with our soul, Divine Flow develops. What we need merges with what we want. Then, things get interesting. Being in a higher frequency, we notice the first small bends in our reality. Little conveniences such as finding lost objects, time standing still so we can make our appointment, being directed to the perfect book for our circumstances, or meeting the right contact. They can easily be dismissed as odd the first time, but when reality bending keeps happening and becomes steeper, we notice. This is evidence we are in Divine Flow. In this, your soul or spirit helpers lend a hand or prompt you to step in a particular direction. They manifest these reality shifts to get your attention. It is unconscious manifestation for our benefit.

Let us go into pretend mode and try on all that we have learned.

Imagine going to work or school. On the way, notice all that you have manifested for your behalf (even though we know we have not consciously manifested anything). When you arrive, notice the details of nature around you, the trees, sky, clouds, grass. Notice the building as you enter and take credit for manifesting its form appearance. Notice the people you encounter. You manifested their presence, each for a particular purpose and reason, which you need not know the specifics of. Notice whether you contract or expand; notice if those around you are expanded or contracted. What could you do or say to change someone or yourself from contraction to expansion? For example, if you tell someone who has their head down (a sign of contraction) that they look stunning today, will that create a shift? They look up, having been noticed and hit with positive energy, and politely smile back and utter gratitude. Gratitude is a higher frequency, and even if they only fake being nice, the fact that someone noticed and complimented them creates a shift. They cannot help but expand. If they are moved, they will expand a lot. Notice if you shift from their reaction. Do you contract in disappointment or expand in delight? Now, you have changed the world by helping yourself and someone else shift energetically, who in turn will influence others you and they meet. You are manifesting and un-manifesting energetically and consciously.

Why is it helpful to know what is collectively, personally, consciously, or unconsciously manifested?

When we get into directing intention, as in healing work, we need clarity on what is at play. Let us say I want to assist someone in remitting cancer. I need to know if the individual manifested the cancer as a lesson or if it had unconsciously manifested as part of a soul contract. That will determine whether healing will be possible and to what degree. Can you look back at events in your life and guess if they were consciously or unconsciously manifested? Can you see where you may have been complicit or responsible? We have wonderful vision in hindsight. Doing this helps clarify the path forward. If I can see what I have created and understand why, I can then understand why I do not need to do that anymore. I can now change my ways. This is using free will to step in the direction of Divine Flow with directions as Divine Will.

Love as Energy

Let's investigate love.

Love is an emotion with an unlimited frequency range.

My late father once manifested before me in pure soul form. He was a vortex of amazing Cassiopeian energy, a frequency I had never experienced before—a crystalline textured frequency of love times 300,000! Of course, though I cannot share what that felt like in words, it was among the most stunning experiences of energy I have ever had. His presence came, in part, to teach me who we are beyond our human form. It set the bar for what I wanted to actualize. I did not want to wait until I died to experience this amazing energy. I told my spiritual team this would be the goal, determined to see it through. With help from a spirit helper, I connected to my soul. I managed to anchor this energy, and to this day, it flows through me. At times, I feel just overwhelmed with gratitude for that being able to happen, but anyone can do this, and when I help you connect to your soul, you will begin to experience this.

This crystalline energy flows through my experience of being. I am flowing through work and home and even driving my car. It starts after breakfast and winds down before bed. Some days, the energy is more intense, or people seem to trigger a bump in frequency. The energy jumps when a client with a lot of trauma comes before me. I have learned to recognize this as the energy of my soul and listen to it. It shows me what excites my soul. Likewise, I can sense what my soul dislikes. It has been a guide with which to be *in* the world. I feel honored to be the co-pilot with my soul. This shows your soul can be experienced in a physical way. It is another bend in our understanding of what is possible.

Mother Teresa's lens is love. Every breath is done with love. Every moment is lived in love. Every action is done lovingly. Doing this changes the frequency we experience.

Masaru Emoto, a Japanese researcher, conducted experiments with water. He put water in jars labeled with different emotions or left some blank. He used emotional labels like "love" or "I hate you." He applied labeled names of music such as John Lennon's "Imagine" or music by Mozart. He examined the water after it froze and photographed the sample's ice crystals under a high-powered microscope. The results are stunning. We clearly see that water responds dramatically differently to different frequencies. The positive energy samples organized into elaborately organized snowflake like patterns, while negative samples were chaotic and disorganized. He saw that thoughts and emotions hold and transmit powerful energy and impact the world around us. Sound familiar? Our bodies are 60 percent water. Thus, if Mother Teresa greets us with love, sees us as love, experiences us as love—imagine what that does to the water molecules in our cells. No wonder people holding negative emotions manifest disease states.

Imagine what you can do, as Mother Teresa suggested, by doing little things with great love. Can we view the world through these spectacles? Can we see others as love? Imagine sending love to the 60 percent water in them to change the frequency of those molecules. But we need to raise our frequency first. The frequency of water is 528hz. Listening to music at 432—528hz—with headphones—will change your frequency. I expect listening to music you enjoy would also have a similar impact. Imagine you are bathing in a tub of water charged with love energy. As you soak in this loving energy bath, drink some cold refreshing water that is also charged with loving emotion. You can have 528hz music playing. Love is 500hz, gratitude is 540hz. Just imagining this is giving the energy an intention, and so it shifts. Stay with this as a meditation. Supercharge your food by envisioning all the benefits it will bestow upon you. You then energize it with a nutritious intention.

Tonglen: Practicing Loving Compassion

As we give and receive love, our frequency increases, and we experience expansion. Visualize being in love. Imagine that frequency increasing by picturing yourself giving and receiving love. You can do this with people, animals, or plants—it does not matter.

Inhale and exhale love. Wait and feel the energy rise.

Now feel the expansion that results. Now repeat this but add to the number of recipients you send and receive love with. Wait. Sense the energy and expansion. Repeat, adding to the number of recipients. Expand beyond specific groups or types. Keep expanding. Send and receive love to global groups such as all the children in the world, all the people, all the fish, plants, wildlife, and so on. Add one global group at a time, then accumulate all together, and send and receive love. Then expand. This is a play on an ancient Tibetan Buddhist practice known as Tonglen.

Tonglen involves a similar process but focuses on the suffering of a loved one and sends healing to them after first inhaling and grounding all their pain. The healing energy we manifest must match the suffering energy. We then expand to two family members, then four, then our whole family. Then we add friends and go on to global groups, increasing the amount of suffering we inhale, feel, and ground, yet also increasing the love and healing energy we send.

The legend around Tonglen goes back to ancient Tibet. A leper colony had been established several mountain ranges away from a village at the foot of the Himalayan Mountains. (Leprosy is a highly contagious disease where patches of body die both internally and externally. It is awful, and civilizations of ancient times developed the idea of a colony to isolate them from afflicting others. Another famous leprosy colony was Molokai in Hawaii.) The village would send someone periodically to check on their leprosy-afflicted loved ones, help in burying the deceased, and gather anything they needed. One day, the person checking on them, after climbing up and down several mountain ranges to get there, was approached by one of the lepers. The leper, whose face was covered in grayish silver blotches, said, "You must leave and never return." Shocked, the villager protested, "What? You cannot ask such a thing. We care about you, and this is the least we can do. How will you get by without some help?" The leper stood their ground and said, "You are putting yourself and our loved ones at risk by coming here. We do not want anyone to suffer as we have, so you must promise to leave and never return. We will take care of ourselves as best as we can. You must promise!" This shocked the villager. He knew he would get slack for agreeing but backed down and consented. He wished them luck and returned to the village.

The villagers were, as expected, appalled at his decision to not return. They said, "We will send someone else if not you." He pleaded, "I gave my word; we must honor that." The villagers then backed down, unhappy with this decision. The lepers developed a group meditation, doing what I described above as Tonglen. They did not want their loved ones to suffer in any way and proceeded to take on their pain, inhaling and grounding it so the families no longer had any suffering left. They then proceeded to send love and healing to match. They expanded into global groups, and after they finished inhaling and sending healing to the whole world, they would simply begin again the next day. They practiced Tonglen as a group daily. Several years went by, and the villagers believed their loved ones would all be deceased. They agreed to send an individual over the mountain ranges to check on the lepers and tend to the last needed burials. As he approached the colony, to his surprise, a large group sat in a circle practicing meditation. He moved in closer so he could see their faces. Their faces were completely clear of the gray patches, the hallmark presence of leprosy.

Can you practice Tonglen on yourself, Inhaling your suffering and sending yourself love and healing?

Being Love

When we have expanded as love and walk down the street, we notice a shift has taken place. No us-them separation occurs. We are both the loved and the lover. We love the world. The world loves us. We are love. This expansion means change. We are change. It circles back to this truth of who we are, but flavored with energy as love. Feel this love energy in the air as you inhale love.

Exhale love and expand.

Now breathe through your skin. Imagine breathing through every skin cell, through every surface skin covers. Exhale through your skin. Continue to do this, breathing through your entire body. Your energy will increase rapidly. This is a Qigong exercise known as full-body breathing. (Bonus: Try doing this while playing the music of Mei-lan Maurits on YouTube. She is a voice channel of Source energy). Feel the love energy and allow it to increase and expand within you. Expand with each cycle of breath until you cannot expand any further. Ask yourself, "Am I beyond definition?" Just as God is beyond definition, we are, in oneness, being beyond definition. We are energy that moves and never stops moving. It cannot be contained, and it has no age or sense of time. It has always been, but we are only now just becoming aware of it. It is eternal.

As you inhale eternity, it fills your lungs. It runs through your veins and into your cells. Eternity becomes you with each cycle of breath. We look around and notice we are timeless within the context of a timeline. The collective has created this timeline, and we comply rather than resist. We still experience ourselves as moving, love energy, as ever-expanding and timeless. We comply with the structure of context, of timeline, though we are not aligned with it. It is not hard to do—to dance within a context that we have done all our life. We know how to do this, only now we vibrate at a higher frequency. We do not need to lower our frequency to comply. It simply feels different. There is no resistance because there is no *I* to do the resisting. It is detached, as we are not aligned with defining contexts or timelines. This becomes more natural-feeling as you acclimate to being at this very high altitude. The eternal love energy we actualize is who we are as a soul within our human form.

When we are passionate about something, we bring energy to it, giving it a charge. People who express their passions often manifest the object they are directing energy to. This is because they manifest this through love.

Love belongs to a higher frequency, meaning it is less dense and can travel faster. Passion is love. Therefore, they literally love what they are passionate about into existence. We can look historically at great accomplishments manifested due to the passion of their creators. We can say these creations were life-long passions of philosophers, artists, inventors, scientists, writers, athletes, explorers, chefs, advocates, or even great parents.

When sixteen-year-old Greta Thunberg pleaded to world leaders at the United Nations to take responsibility for our climate change, her speech held pure passion. The passion of her speech enabled her message to be heard worldwide. Passion can be applied to your healing and ultimate ascension. In fact, it must be. If we are to move the goalpost from stagnation to movement, we need to energize with passion and compassion. We must commit—200 percent.

How do you know if you are passionate about something?

You know because you love it. You may have passion for the work you do or for being of service to our beloved planet and its cohabitants. Earlier, we released our passion, as the target was egoic connection, self-identity. No doubt many famous people who passionately manifested their dreams may have done so as egos, but now, in awareness, we can use passion as code for love energy. It is a higher form of being passionate. We must inject passion into our healing process to honor our commitment to learning who we are in truth. We can celebrate who we are *as* truth. We can choose to not do this hard work, but we'll replay our lessons and perpetuate our suffering. That is free will and truly your own choice.

Divine Will is stepping forward from behind the curtain. You are reading this because Divine Will is prompting you to make a passionate choice out of urgency. We can become passionate about releasing what is not true to discover who we are in authenticity. Our urgent passion drives us down the path of healing and manifesting what is true. Truth is distilled as the raw base of our existence.

When we add passion to whatever we are doing, we add love. If we are passionate about cooking, we are in love with cooking. If we are a passionate fan, we are in love with the team and what they do. Love belongs to a higher frequency, so when we are passionate, we move ourselves to a higher place, though we may not be aware of doing so. Any time we move the frequency needle upward, we are more likely to affect another. They sense our energy and get excited with us. This raises their vibration as well.

Have you ever been inspired by someone? You take on that passion and allow yourself to also rise in frequency. When we bring others along by lifting them in any way, be it intentional or by happenstance, we act in service to them. We also act in service to the collective whole of humanity, as we all benefit from the collective sum of higher frequencies available. When you work through challenges with passion and lift to a higher frequency, you impact those around you. When you simply add an awareness lens to recognize your egoic self-suffering, you are in service. You take a step toward healing, and wanting to heal is self-compassion. We want to heal, to be out of pain, and not experience fear or shame. It is normal to avoid pain, though some of us find maladaptive ways to do that. We can honor those attempts to not suffer without accepting the behavior. Using drugs and alcohol carries a negative stigma because in avoiding our pain by using, we risk hurting others. Despite this, we can honor its intent to not have our Egoic-I suffer. That demonstrates compassion.

Being in service is an act of love. Being passionate or compassionate is an act of love. Do you see where this is going? The truth of our soul's identity is love. As ego, as a separate self, I need to be loved. In realization, I *am* love. All the truths point to identifying our soul as love. We are our soul manifested as human. We are love as our soul-self within our human form. Love as a frequency has no limit; it's infinite in range. It has many shades, many flavors and textures, yet it is all unmistakably love. Everyone is embodied with a soul that is love.

Change

We individually manifest against a backdrop of what is *collectively* manifested.

Collective manifestations include things common to us all, such as the sky, the climate, or our immediate physical environment. We individually manifest within that collective context. It experiences shifts in energy, expansions, contractions, manifesting, and un-manifesting—ongoing, as if there was no time. We manifest the timeline for context. We do not really need a timeline, but for work and living, it really helps.

In higher consciousness, in higher dimensions, this is the case as well. Change happens faster, as energy has less density in dimensions of higher frequency. Change occurs in the context of what is collectively congruent at that frequency. What we ultimately experience, however, depends on a variable.

That variable is what we, as individuals, are able and ready to experience. Some people have more developed abilities, such as being clairaudient, clairvoyant, claircognizant, telepathic, or clairsentient. Some may have multiple abilities to experience with. Some may not be as progressed in their ascension and so may be limited in what they can know or realize. But if we are patient and diligent, such changes will develop, sometimes rapidly. We change constantly within our physical and multidimensional contexts, always in motion.

This may feel like standing on quicksand!

It has always been this way, except now we consciously *experience* life and interrelate with others in this new context of change and impermanence. Nothing we experience is static. Even scientific research has gradually been uncovering that atoms' smallest parts have smaller moving parts and that nothing is ever truly still. We must use this information to avoid letting situations define us. In this way, we must not let *others* define us. We must not let disease or disability or any challenge define us. We must see that, in this paradigm, we are beyond definition.

If we attempt to hang onto an identity, just know that it will be temporary. Change marches on and does not stop. This knowledge surrenders the Egoic-I. In this paradigm, no separate identity is required. There is no separateness, as everything is interrelated and interdependent, energetically connected, and moving. It seems ironic, as, when we look out at our world, it appears so static. If we keep looking, though, we see how the wind moves the leaves, how our body gently moves as we breathe. The shadow on the wall moves. If you trace its edge with a pencil and check it a minute later, you will see it shifted. Everything shifts, including you—your body, your energy, your eyes as they move across this page, your realization of soul within.

The experience of *being change* is realizing the need for limitation no longer exists, even as an idea. It is, at best, a preconception we can transcend because nothing remains static regardless of its solid form appearance. When we stare at the hour and minute arms of a clock, they do not appear to be moving, but they always tick onward. We need not perceive change as evidence we are change, though I know our Egoic-I requires such evidence—at least initially.

When you woke up this morning, did you feel the same as yesterday morning or the morning before? You will probably feel different at the end of the day than you felt at the start of the day or at noon. Notice your breathing and the movement necessary for breathing to occur. As you notice these movements, can you feel your heart beating? It is you who is moving. It is you who changes, just like the clock hands. Perhaps not so apparently, but absolutely, nonetheless.

As change, what is possible?

If we can understand that everything is impermanent, we can be empowered. Our capacity is no longer limited to the word *possible*, which suggests a limit or boundary. We can see we do not need such limiting language. These ideas and our attachments to them can be realized as illusionary. For example: You cannot be worthless if you are not an *I*. Worthlessness is an egoic identity of limitation. It suggests a limitation in what we can do, what we can receive, who we can be in relationship with, and when no such walls contain us. There are no such restrictions. They only exist in the fixed world of the Egoic-I.

Egoic-I cannot live in the world of expansion or change. The world of expansion or change stays in this moment and does not require thought. In contrast, Egoic-I must have thought and a reference to the past, to a timeline. Change and movement are only noticed in the context of time. However, the timeline does not extend to our past. It just remains present enough to provide a context so that we can recognize movement. We are still learning, so allow time to be in the background. Going through the day without a timeline helps us be more aware. Noticing expansion, contraction, or what consciously manifests, or un-manifests, helps us be in the lens of awareness.

As *change*, we are not definable.

Who are we?

We are trillions of atoms, just like the trillions of stars in the universe. In each atom, electrons and protons move rapidly.

"I celebrate myself, and sing myself, and what I assume you shall assume. For every atom belonging to me as good belongs to you." — *Walt Whitman, Song of Myself*.[8]

The same carbon atoms make up everything we experience, as we are the same, yet different. Perhaps we have more or fewer atoms, but all before us relates more to us than we realize. We are, in truth, no different nor separate from all that is. All is in a state of motion—everything changes, evolves, or devolves. We are one with change. We are not separate from change or anything that changes.

All is energy.

We are energy that forever moves, flows, and shifts, just as all before us. It energetically flows and shifts despite its illusionary, static appearance.

Play and Creativity

When we surrender the context of victimhood, micro-timelines, and self-identification, we can be free, open, and expanded.

We can still do our jobs and be in relationships. We can still love, play, and create. If you do not love, play, or create, perhaps you should start here. If you grew up and were denied a normal childhood, play may be foreign to you. It may take some exploring as to how you can

---

8   Walt Whitman, The Complete Poems, ed. Francis Murphy (Baltimore: Penguin Books, 1975), 63.

even manifest a fun experience. You'll need to make up for lost time, as play is essential.

We observe animals in the wild, naturally playing as young, expressing freedom and silliness. Their parents must set limits for their safety, as they are not yet aware of any boundaries to their playfulness. In our experiencing play, there is nothing serious, just fun and playful exploring.

Think of what you miss doing or would like to initiate. You may need to adapt that idea, as you are bigger now and structures are different. When children play, they activate their imagination. Imagination frees us and combined with play, enables us to enjoy our now moment in a new way. In playing with imagination, we suspend our internal permission system as to what we can imagine.

If we allow ourselves to have fun and play with this, we can develop certain skills. Fun lives in a higher energy, so we get a bump in frequency, but we also exercise our ability to see creatively. It is playing in the world, free of the limiting concept of *possible*. This is a wonderful place to initiate creativity.

Being creative puts play to form. It manifests our imagination so it can be shared with others. It can be art, cooking, dance, writing, movement, performing, visualizing, and creating in ways not listed. Creators get blocked when they take creating too seriously. To unblock, they need to surrender all expectation regarding outcomes. It does not matter what the outcome is, especially when we first start. The idea is to be a kid and make a mess of whatever it is. Know from the start that the outcome will be discarded. It is about the process, not the product. This frees us of hidden permissions and ideas of judgment, as if some mystery person will walk in and judge us. Do not allow anyone to judge your experience of playing, as this will just shut things down. This needs to be your private experience so you can be free. When you create playfully, you will see creativity flow. Experimenting with imagination in playful creation entertains us and moves us away from context and timelines. We, in a sense, take a vacation from all other processes we engage with in the world.

We can play with experiencing this freedom—this limitlessness with joy. If you enjoy the process, then it can become a passion. Doing it daily, as a ritual, with time set aside just for this, will assist in your ascension. I was encouraged to paint daily after meditating without expectation. I was instructed to get out of the way—that means no ego. I just took paint on wet watercolor paper and splashed color on it. I went with whatever I felt like doing. It did not matter if it was not art; it was about playing like a little kid. I could make a mess as I explored and had fun. It did not matter. I timed the ritual for thirty minutes. The process morphed into a spiritual experience over time, as it was practice in not being egoic. It reinforced that process of not engaging "I."

I ended up painting via channeled energies through my body that directed the process. My guides or Higher Self did the creating, and my body simply facilitated. Herb lent some art school info in, and the results were energy vortex-laden paintings. The cover of this book is one of those energy emitting paintings. Hold in in front of you and you will feel a vortex of energy it emits! It tricked my mind to allow me to be free. Eventually, I had over 300 paintings. I edited them and ended up displaying twenty-five at once at an art show at my local library in Huntington, NY.

Play and creativity help us realize freedom from contextual identity and timelines and allows us to realize nothing is fixed. We have assigned a permanence to those structures in the past.

Nothing is permanent, and in releasing this false idea, we see that everything changes.

Freedom

By now, hopefully you have flirted with the taste of freedom.

It is expansive by nature and immensely empowering. It does not empower in an egoic sense, however, as it assists in our escape from the egoic prison. Freedom is not needing permission to feel or do what we truly want. It is being able to do nothing and be all right with it. There are no mandates, contexts, or timelines. Being free to be without restriction or limitation allows us to celebrate *being*.

We can celebrate our breath. We celebrate expansion and contraction. We celebrate darkness, and its equal in light. In stillness, we notice and celebrate movement, manifesting out of non-movement before our eyes. We celebrate intention as the action within inaction. We are in realization. Everything manifests or un-manifests without end, regardless of our awareness of such. The realization helps keep the prison doors open. We can see the contexts as illusion. Freedom is realizing there is no purpose for falsely believing that a prior identity would define our life purpose.

We live and exist beyond all definition. *That* is freedom because when we are beyond definition, we expand. We cannot focus on capacity or what is possible because we are beyond such words. If this is becoming too abstract, just let go and be, breathe and be your breath. Connect this moment of fleeting freedom to other moments of fleeting freedom until they all merge into the constant connected experience.

Freedom as a Self-Identified Experience

Limitations appear as form so the dance of manifesting and un-manifesting form can commence. We need illusionary timelines and contexts to facilitate egoic participation in the world. We know, through a different lens, that these structures are inherently empty, and as movement, I cannot not be threatened by them, as no *me* really exists. I accept the collective agreements and dance as others require but have no attachment to their ideas of who I need to be, as I am beyond such definition.

Stephen Hawking was wheelchair-bound because of a degenerative disease. He depended on another person just to go to the bathroom. He could not deny such a harsh limitation. He accepted his limitation as part of his life rather than as a self-defeating identity. He refused to have his capacity defined by any limitation. He chose freedom as a view. As a physicist, he understood change from a scientific perspective rather than a spiritual one. Hawking was able to get to that same lens of freedom to peer through.

Emotions are said to be thoughts embodied. Thus, since emotions are energy, we can say thoughts convert to energy and re-manifest as emotions in form. Take this abstract intellectual banter about freedom and bring it into your body as *knowing*. This converts it to energy. Wear it as I share with you more about a similar experience.

The slave, Anna Brown, did eventually shed her label of slave after the Civil War. Yet the freedom she found started almost twenty years prior to that. Her realization did not remove the leg iron from her ankle, nor did it stop her owners from continuing to define her as property. In realization, she did not need to experience the rancid taste they offered. She stopped ingesting the "rotten food." She, in the state of knowing, redefined herself as *eternally* free and could see that her suffering became unnecessary. She remained enslaved and treated as such, but she accepted this facade as temporary. She could not be defined in this way anymore. She understood the purpose it served (to look inward rather than outward) and released the rancidness and the lies it told. She lived in truth, and the truth felt good, unlike rancid.

When we free ourselves of suffering, we shift our experience of the world. The form appearance may still look the same, but we can no longer taste the rancidness. We now can taste freedom and shift. Freedom as a *knowing* becomes a truth. It has always been so.

As freedom, we redefine our world. We no longer attach ourselves to self-defining structures. We merely see and experience them, just as young Anna felt that leg iron that was too small digging into her ankle. It did not concern her. It had nothing to do with who she was. The people and structures that choose to tell us who we are or how much we are worth have no idea who we really are. They see a form appearance when they look in our direction—an appearance which manifested solely to experience this reality. This appearance barely contains our radiant, true self, nor does it reflect all the movement and change. Our form appearance does not reveal the multidimensional impact we have at this moment by just being. We allow them to dance and spin, as they only know this limited view. As freedom, we can accept them as they are, but we no longer accept the definitions they offer. They are no longer needed. We know who we are in knowing, as truth—as free from all definition.

Only a few days after writing this, I came across an editorial published in *The Washington Post Weekly* titled "This Holiday Season, We Can All Learn a Lesson from Beethoven." Arthur C. Brooks provided a history lesson about Beethoven. The composer and performer had already risen to fame by the time he reached twenty. His hearing, however, had faded rapidly, and eventually he became completely deaf. He stopped performing and destroyed pianos by banging the keys so hard in attempt to hear something. He stopped composing and eventually realized he had to adapt. He found he could put a pencil in his mouth and feel the vibrations of notes. He lost his ability to hear other contemporary musicians' work and therefore lost the ability to be influenced by them. He became an island, composing only what he imagined his music would sound like. The result was music that was unique for the time and revolutionized the direction of music.[9]

His greatest string quartets and the famous "Ninth Symphony" were created by a Beethoven who couldn't hear a note.

The point?

His limitation created a path to realize total creative freedom. Freedom allows us to experiment with new possibilities and new ways

---

9   Brooks, Arthur C. "This holiday season, we can all learn a lesson from Beethoven." *Washington Post*. December 13, 2019. https://www.washingtonpost.com/opinions/this-holiday-season-we-can-all-learn-a-lesson-from-beethoven/2019/12/13/71f21aba-1d0e-11ea-b4c1-fd0d91b60d9e_story.html

to frame our experience of being or creating like Beethoven did. We cannot be afraid of change if we *are* change!

Being free offers adjustment, acclimating to different frequencies. It changes our experience of being in the world. What matters shifts. I think so I may function and make decisions, but I am still unattached to any ideas of self. I remain as change, a form that manifests and un-manifests, expands and contracts unceasingly.

Greta Thunberg was asked if her Asperger's Syndrome challenged or limited her. She replied, "I have Aspergers Syndrome, and that means I'm sometimes a bit different from the norm, and given the right circumstance—being different is a superpower."[10] She elaborated and said she views herself as having "superpowers." Now *that* is reframing a limiting belief.

Our human form acts as a temporary temple in which we can worship our humanness and adjoin the world that we helped manifest in oneness. As energy, we are love, and it is just a matter of getting out of the way to realize that. As love, we are a projector. We project love out to the world, and that energy manifests into form. Love comes back to us again and again. We are one with all we have been complicit in manifesting, as well as one with all that has been collectively manifested. Our individual energies will impact and shift the collective, but we must be patient.

The more people project love, the more impact on the collective. In this way, we can change the world. We can join Greta and use our superpowers to help Earth realize the best version of itself. We realize our superpowers when we lose the limitations of self-definition. This

---

10   Maija Fappler, "Gretta Thunberg on Being Different is a Superpower," Huffington Post Australia Article Archive, September 21, 2019. https://Huffpost.com/archive/au/entry/greta-thunberg-on-having-aspergers-being-different-is-a-superpower_au_5db0644e40cdfe05733161.

is exactly what Greta did. Thank you, Greta! She defies definition, and when she has been attacked, she brushes it off as nothing—no ego buttons on display. She points to a better Earth. With urgency and passion, she is one individual seeking to impact the collective. Likewise, each of us, in our own way, can join in helping the collective shift.

Greta is fearless.

Beethoven was brave.

We need not be a Greta or a Beethoven and feel such immense responsibility. We may not have such big limitations to release or work through. Finding our freedom will just be simpler and easier. Listening and taking directions from our heart replaces following the rancid taste to learn and grow. We transmute not having abilities that someone else has by accepting we are exactly where we need to be at this moment.

Accept that we know what we need to know for now—a sacred moment of a complete and total state of unconditional acceptance.

THOSE WHO ARE NOT FREE

Through the lens of freedom, we can see others spinning, limited by their myopic view and unnecessary self-limiting beliefs. We also become acutely aware of others' suffering. What is our role now that we feel free of such suffering? Are we responsible? We're certainly not responsible for the work others must do to learn their own lessons. It would not help to take those lessons away, even to remove suffering.

As a trauma therapist, I do not heal others. I facilitate them in healing themselves. I respect it is *their* journey. Energy healers can accomplish this kind of healing, and I have done such work with energy. It just means the lessons will need to re-manifest at another time or timeline. It is seductive to have such abilities—it undoubtedly feels good to instantly remove an obstacle causing suffering. I have learned to use discretion, but I am aware of other spiritual intuitive healers who are apparently unaware of the consequences that may result from quick fixes. We can prompt someone in the direction of addressing a lesson. We can suggest moving past or show how their maladaptive avoidance is keeping them stuck. In our view, we may have insight into what is happening.

We may need to sit on that as the lesson plays out. It may mean letting someone fail. It may be their path, and if learning must occur, it is okay for us to be on the sidelines as observers. We can help with gentle feedback like, "That does not seem to be working out for you the way you would like." Sometimes people do not realize they have a choice. They feel hopeless and stuck because, in that egoic view, they are unable to realize what is possible. From our lens, we can prompt energetic change and expansion from their contracted state. We then point to changes in experience that may suggest moving beyond hopelessness. I can see the collective has manifested separateness and prioritized profit over seeking causal-based permanent solutions. I can see what is possible if the collective shifted. I need to allow that the collective is not yet ready. I must sit and let this dance play out. But I can poke and call attention to what is beyond possible to point to another idea that feels good.

I have been shown the Earth and four streams of light moving around it, symbolizing four layers of shift. In meditation, I then saw a shoebox of old print photos, symbolic of the past. But when I lifted each photograph to view it, each was blank on both sides. That suggests that the past will not be in our future.

Life on Earth will be very different in 2035. Earth has a soul, and it too is ascending.

After shifting is completed, we will be, as a human collective, enjoying an Earth where separateness, hatred, and greed no longer exist. We are already going through these shifts on this planet, which may explain why things feel so awful or confusing. The good news is that we are in the first phase of possibly five. Our self-realization is part of this shift.

Finding Our Purpose

How do we find our purpose?

Our purpose here refers to why we, as a soul, have taken on a human incarnation. It may or may not overlap with what we do as a financial occupation. We are here to learn lessons and self-actualize as a soul. Beyond that, we have a reason to be, currently, with the people we share being with. Our ultimate reason to adjoin others on planet Earth is to be in service. How this manifests is individual to you. It can seem abstract because service may take many forms, some of which are subtle. If you connect casually to someone in passing and that transient contact manifests expansion, *that* is service. If we are conscious and act with intention, we energetically supercharge the act. This casual moment transforms into a higher purpose, as our intention is to help this individual to expand. We expand as a reaction, and that person, in their expanded form, may cause others to expand. It's a chain reaction. Our small intention ends up having a big consequence, and we may not even be aware of it.

Our soul's purpose is revealed by our soul, and thus you will need to work and develop a relationship with your soul to reveal both your soul's purpose and your Divine Plan. Your soul's purpose is unique to your soul and has had the same purpose over time and through each of its many incarnations and different soul origins. Our Divine Purpose is what we do to operationalize our Divine Plan, revealed to us by our soul. Our Divine Purpose and soul purpose may be two different purposes, but it will most likely be closely related if not the same. For example: I am taking the idea of working as a trauma therapist to a more global reach to create a greater transformation via writing books, making videos, and participating in speaking engagements. I learned this was my Divine Plan but later learned my soul's purpose (via my soul) is to be an alchemist. Transformation and alchemy are not unsimilar.

DIVINE FEMININE, DIVINE MASCULINE

Our Divine Purpose reflects the Divine Feminine, or Christ Consciousness. We are love, and as love, we expand to others and to all things. The compassion for all that is does not exclude compassion for us. The Divine Masculine, inner strength, enables the Divine Feminine to manifest. We can see how this flavor tastes different from the unenlightened masculine, with its fear-based patriarchal power and control.

You can experience the energies of the Divine Masculine and the Divine Feminine in Amorah Quan Yin's *The Pleiadean Workbook: Awakening Your Divine Ka*. Power and control, which drives patriarchy, prevail in government, religious institutions, business structures, and family cultures. It is egoic—based on fear and separateness. But if we embrace the concept of the Divine Masculine and Divine Feminine, we act in service. If we help humanity realize these states, our planet will evolve and be a peaceful and sustainable place to inhabit. We will someday experience society in a balance of Divine Feminine and Divine Masculine, not patriarchy nor matriarchy. I cannot tell you, beyond these ideas, what your Divine Purpose specifically is. As you open to receiving direction from your soul, you will be prompted to serve your Divine Purpose.

Divine Flow directs us through our Divine Plan, and eventually we realize our Divine Purpose. Through this, we can work to actualize as much as possible in our lifetime. If we passionately work in Divine Flow, Divine Purpose self-manifests. Obviously, not everyone will get so far as to realize their soul's purpose for being. Our soul is eternal for this very reason—it can take many lifetimes to evolve such a purpose. When we do become aware of our purpose, we can use urgency to bring passion to our actions. That energizes our intention and helps drive our purpose home.

When a dog is in pain, if we approach it, it may snap at us even though it knows us. It does not know what to do with its pain and suffering. It does not know we are not associated with it, so it snaps to protect. It does not want to hurt us, but it does not know how else to be and deal with pain. We see humans snap at each other or be mean. They are in pain and suffering. They are not self-aware, nor are they taking responsibility, so they blame others for their discomfort. Instead of judging them, we can allow ourselves to let the Divine Feminine prevail and instead see them with compassion. See that they are like this hurt dog who does not know what to do with its pain.

Servicing God, Earth, and Humanity requires both passion and compassion, and our passion and compassion are urgently needed. Now.

Explore your world now—inhale and notice.

You have so much to consider. This depends on where you stand in your journey. You may have so many options. Can you incorporate the Divine Masculine and Divine Feminine as shifts in being? Imagine inner strength growing inside your core. Feel or imagine compassion energy in your heart center, empowered by this inner strength so that this love for all things gets stronger and more powerful. Let it explode and blow apart any boundaries attempting to contain it.

Be radiant!

Can you incorporate urgency, passion, and compassion in what you are doing, regardless of where you may be? Moving into these shifts as they feel good moves us closer to our purpose, as well as our experience as a soul, as our experience of being sacred.

Deepening Surrender

It may be beneficial to ponder these concepts, trying them on experientially, in a daily meditation practice.

Try integrating these ideas by just doing a daily routine, only with new awareness and a deeper sense of being conscious. This lens of being presently conscious allows us to see ourselves in awareness or ego and pulls us back to see the big picture. What tastes rancid becomes obvious, though the solutions may not be. Be patient, and if you can hold on to this view, answers will present. Surrender to trust, and experiment with the risk of trusting. In this, we ask our soul to show the way.

Our soul knows, as it has the best view. It knows all time and knows what is possible. We ask and trust that an answer will manifest. Do not descend into expectation (ego), but rather ask, and be open to whatever presents, however it presents, whenever it presents. You may not be ready to "hear," but will perhaps be prompted or have your path hinted to you. The reason for this indirect process, initially, is that we need to show, via free will, that we want to move in a direction away from suffering. Our soul, as Higher Self, wants evidence that we are committed to change. The more we act in free will to remove sources of rancid, the more trust develops between us and our Higher Self. Eventually, there will not be separation between us and our Higher Self. This shows up as "trusting our gut."

You can help manifest this answer by focusing on it in meditation. Do not suppress self-talk. Allow some back and forth in your mind, and this becomes a path for new information to sneak in, try automatic writing, that is write your question and what you receive without pausing to think. Just keep writing and flow will manifest.. It is shocking how much was transmitted to me without me being aware of it. There were no grand announcements, and initially I was not able to discern the mental voice from thought—the same as my own and my Higher Self. I still acknowledge I am more of a receiver than I know.

When we move from the egoic lens to the awareness lens to the soul lens, we lose that defined sense of ourselves. That comfort gets sacrificed for unlimited expansion. This is letting go, letting go completely. I am surprised I do not miss self-identifying and no longer find it purposeful, but we must eventually realize that possibility has no rules. Miracles no longer seem miraculous because the context of impossibility has been lifted. You probably feel some resistance to this reality as you read. We have walked through much reality bending and now step into a deeper part of the pool. We notice our feet no longer touch the bottom, and we briefly panic.

You will not sink, but that's only realized when you are ready. It requires a complete release of trust as a concept. The slightest trust issue still has attachment to ego. It is work worth pursuing, but you may also require outside help to transmute any subtle, remaining trust issues. I have found these can be deeply embedded and difficult to even be conscious of, but I know of the presence of such through the resistance to opening to, using, or realizing abilities. Sampling, tasting, or easing in may be a path for some, while others may just jump in. Then, the issue of validation comes up. Is this really happening? When reality bends frequently, it becomes less of an issue, but if we realize we are the bender, it seems like a drastically different idea. It creates a new definition that no longer has clear rules regarding our relationship to what we know as *real*. This is working in higher consciousness. It has a looser set of rules, as energy manifesting form can happen in an instant. Everything is energy. It happens before our eyes, manifested by mere intention. It happens if this is for the highest good, as that is higher energy.

We live with the unlimited potential to move beyond this 3D experience and heal, change, and create in ways we could not possibly imagine. We can co-create with God. And God wants and needs our help, so God lends a hand. Reality bends and we freak out. We freak out because we ask, "Do I deserve to hold hands with God?"

This may frighten or overwhelm us, but as the truth settles in, we feel nothing but love. We do not need to fear love, just as we do not need to fear God, or the concept of God, or the possibility of being one with God. Holding hands with God is swimming in the deep end. We realize we are no longer who we thought we were as we exist beyond mind or any mentation of such thought-derived definition. Let go and accept God's loving hand, the help, and the bend as you realize there is nothing you cannot do.

In the deep end, in over our head, we instinctively want to act. Try to surrender to trusting, as we will float no matter what. Surrender to a new idea about surrendering. See trust and surrender as completely as possible. We will lose our boundaries and become one with God—one with all that is. We are the energy of being, and as that energy, anything is possible.

From this point on, know you are not alone. You will be loved, taken care of, and helped in discovering your divine life purpose, as well as in manifesting its actualization. Here, free will lies before you in a way you may not be familiar with. You do not have to do this alone. You can use free will to ask for assistance and to express gratitude for such.

Writing this book is a perfect example. I know this is a Divine Purpose I am here to provide, and hopefully humanity will benefit from the words presented. As I proceeded deeper into the book, I noticed I had no idea what I would write. I had to trust that content would materialize as I simultaneously became student, author, and teacher. The process requires me to not resist, to surrender, and to know that what I write answers my call for assistance. I will write today as I will write tomorrow, even though I have no idea where this text will go next. I am in over my head with you! But I know there is no drowning, only floating higher and higher as I hold God's hand lovingly and imagine that whisper, "You are not alone. I am here to help."

I don't hear anything. I don't see anything.

Reality bending before our eyes is evidence enough! We want evidence and validation. The words you read now are evidence of such. When I write that I don't understand, it is then explained to me. I am having a live conversation with God, my Higher Self, or whoever is providing this material.

This book is a guide for wherever you are at, and I do not expect everyone to be at the same stage of readiness going forward. Everyone, please accept that we all move at the pace we can handle. We are not lesser-than if it takes longer than another to move along our path. This text means to provide a reframing of such a journey, with tools and guideposts to map out the path and to show we can use the lessons of our life, regardless of how traumatic, to move onto a path of ascension and realizing who we are in truth.

We have learned that we can view our immediate experience of being through three lenses, each one manifesting a different paradigm of reality. We see there are structures in place for us to use or abandon as needed. Such structures include ego, suffering, timelines, awareness, energy, emptiness and form, knowing, change, manifestation, truth, expansion and contraction, passion, freedom, and surrender. We have free will to engage with these structures in a way that can mobilize us to evolve to the highest possible version of ourselves. Engaging in lesson learning is stepping into an ascension journey, though, at first, our priority is to move away from suffering. It is a natural progression toward healing. After we move away from pain, we can start to feel a shift as our world changes in response to the hard work we put forth. Now, we can plug in these structures. Now, we can choose which lens and what structure to use. We empower ourselves to be agents of change instead of victims. We have free will to decide whether we want to walk the path of ascension or not. This may not be the path that resonates with you. It may need a different frame, or perhaps this is not the time or lifetime to do this. Free will exists to honor us with the power to choose.

We will look at the different role free will plays compared to Divine Will, but first let us dive deeper into the world we create to have purpose in and how that happens.

Free Will Versus Divine Will

Through our free will, we may choose to continue manifesting experiences that justify fear and limitation. Or we can choose to use this free will to move in a different direction.

Free will is our wild card. We must learn our contracted lessons as a soul, but free will also give us the ability to choose how, how soon, and what lens to experience the world through. We can use free will to influence what manifests and un-manifests or to move beyond contracted lessons. In free will, we choose to expand or contract. We could choose to change frequencies or not. You see how powerful you really are?

If we engage in free will, we are free to make decisions, but from an egoic lens, we can choose to sustain fear and limitation. We can choose to avoid *rancid* by drinking, drugging, or through some other avoidant behavior. We can also use free will to make decisions that honor our commitment to self-realize.

Free will is truly free.

Divine Will is surrendering to what is in alignment with our Divine Plan. Our Divine Plan is all the lessons we came here to learn, in respect to soul realization. It is then our soul's plan to evolve. As we notice what is rancid, and explore the source, expose, and release rot, we do the work of our Divine Plan. This is the divinity of atrocity, as atrocity has a purpose, or it would not exist. We have an opportunity to learn and evolve. Choosing this path works toward your Divine Plan, thus aligning with Divine Will. Within our free will, we choose to align. After we get through all the big lessons, the big traumas, the big relationships, the job changes, the adjustments to life and work, and the healthcare challenges, we can consider *surrender*. The big lessons take so much focus and energy and are worthy of such. Let us not discount the importance of doing that work because we are advancing through this place in the text. It does not mean we cannot align with Divine Will at the same time.

Surrendering to Divine Will does not surrender our sovereignty, rather it empowers it with choice. We pause and become still. We listen and sense. We open to intuitive learning. That is our soul talking. I have plans to meet someone, but a bad feeling comes up. Noticing and listening to that works with our intuition. Trusting intuition is surrendering to Divine Will. Our soul wants you to realize it. It begins with becoming still and paying attention to those subtle shifts, noticing what feels good versus more subtle versions of rancid. As we slip into this noticing and act with such internal guidance, we start to align with Divine Will, by choice, using free will.

We can light up this unconsciously manifested world by bringing a positive intention for every being we meet and assuming a worthy, loving soul resides in each—regardless of whether the person realizes such. We can intend love for each and energetically manifest instead of our usual judging and labeling. This is a step toward oneness and doing so expands us energetically and raises our frequency. It engages Divine Will. We are in service and can manifest that intention to each breath, each action we take.

You can apply this imaginary scenario at home with family. I can recall a recent event where a lesson manifested before my eyes, and I was conscious of it. I had a day off and a long to-do list that I felt eager to get through. On my way home from one errand, I sat behind a stopped truck, waiting to make a left on a road that was a single lane in each direction. I could feel myself becoming impatient (ego) and could hear a whisper, *Be patient* (soul). I saw there was enough room to pass on the right if I just borrowed a little bit of sidewalk. My impulse to do it overpowered all, and in an instant, I hit the gas, and as I drove over the sidewalk. .. BANG. .. POP! I hit a newly manifested pothole and blew out my front tire! Immediately, I became aware of the lesson before me, which manifested as I defied (free will) my internal guidance to be patient (Divine Will). No coincidences—just reality bending ultimately for our benefit.

Arts, Music, Creativity

When I stand before an original Van Gogh painting, I experience a shift.

I am transported energetically, and it is difficult to describe with words. I have experienced this at times when listening intently to music. I have also experienced it when I have read certain poetry, or watched a dance performance, or live performances of various kinds. I have experienced this shift when creating.

Where are we when that moment is happening? What lens are we experiencing? It does not feel ego-like, as it does not self-reference. We are using awareness to get there, but awareness is a neutral experience, and this is not neutral. As an experience, it feels extraordinary and beyond definition. Sound familiar? We are stepping into our soul lens. Our energy changes, and we feel moved in an indescribable way. It feels good, but we cannot put our finger on it. It is too abstract, too unlike anything for which we have language. When we experience being so moved by the arts or music, we experience the energetic expression of our soul. Our soul is energy, and it tells us that it likes this experience. Our soul gets excited and energetically expresses energy. We are tasting our soul.

You may discover creating or experiencing music or arts to be part of your purpose. In an earlier chapter, I suggested playing creatively just to have fun with being in the process. No outcome, just process. This is a way anyone can experience creativity and avoid judgment. I am creative with painting and photography, but I also love music. I cannot play music (well), though I have tried. I have bought a RAV Vast tongue drum, as this is an instrument anyone can play. It does not have any harsh notes, and so when I play, I play like a kid might. I can experiment with its beautiful tones and enjoy its vibrations. I do not perform before anyone. It is just for playtime, but it is creating. It allows the creative process to take over and energetically manifests its own frequency, just as when I paint. There may be other ways you experience this beyond literal arts, such as in cooking or engineering. It may be going for a deep swim in abstract mathematics. I would not want to put an exclusive on what your soul gets excited by.

I heard an extraordinary story on the radio, on WCBS AM, a news report just prior to Thanksgiving. The Handel and Haydn Society had just completed "Mozart's Masonic Funeral Music" at Boston Symphony Hall. A momentary pause passed before the audience erupted with applause. Breaking this silence was a long and deeply expressive "Wooow!!" from a young voice. It was so sincere and moving that it shook the art director, so he set out to find the young "wow" kid. After sending thousands of emails out, he received a response from Stephen Mattin, who had treated his nine-year-old grandson, Ronan, to the concert. It was Ronan who released the wow. Ronan is a non-verbal autistic child. Prior to this event, he had rarely uttered a word.[11]

Perhaps that "wow" was a moment where a word pegged that soul experience. We can say that the conscious experience through creative expression is energetically of our soul. It is divine in nature as our soul is one with God. Thus, we see a spiritual element in art.

Beethoven, Mahler, and others were deeply spiritual. Van Gogh, Kandinsky, Rothko, Michelangelo, and others were also very spiritual and consciously created with spirit. I could go on, but you see the point. Art connects us to the experience of our soul as divinity. Creating art, experiencing art, and consciously realizing that this is the divinity of our soul can help us ascend and evolve. We can consciously deepen our awareness and enjoyment of this energy—of this wow moment.

This serves as a wonderful connection to the energetic voice of our soul within this dimension. I mentioned we can change what we filter as conscious experience. I suggest listening to a vocalist, Mei-lan, who channels via her voice.

At higher dimensions, such as 4D or 5D, we can tune into both beings and information in energetic form.

---

11   Steve Hartman, "A Young Concertgoer Yelled "Wow!". His Grandfather Was More Surprised Than Anyone," CBS News, November 22, 2019, www.cbsnews.com/news/a-young-concertgoer-yelled-wow-his grandfather-was-more-surprised-than-anyone/.

The Others

At higher frequencies, we start to open our awareness of being multi-dimensional. The experience of being on Earth as a human incarnate changes when we realize the presence and influences of other beings.

We do not come into this world alone.

We are provided help that we can recognize if we are able to tune our frequency high enough to make the connection. This sounds scary, but some of these beings in the spirit world are assigned to be with us for life, assist our Higher Self (the energy body of our soul) in our work, and help us realize who we are. Spirit guides, mentors, and teachers all follow us and only intervene if our life is at risk or if we ask for help.

We need to acknowledge before asking, and that requires cutting through self-doubt and increasing trust in what is beyond our understanding of what is possible. When I have helped trauma survivors connect to their spirit guides in my office, they often ask their guides about their life of suffering. "Why haven't you helped?"

The guide answers, "You didn't ask."

Our free will is respected and will not be violated, which allows us to struggle and learn from it. We are free to learn lessons and evolve. We must be the ones to learn our truth. Spirit helpers can assist in pointing things out, but they cannot change the lesson's purpose or core idea. The hard stuff falls on us, with or without their help.

Spirit teams work energetically and can bend the reality we experience to help us get the idea of a lesson or to help validate that they exist. They advise us. Often, we ignore their efforts to help, but not necessarily because we choose to ignore them. We simply don't realize their attempts to communicate, as we don't understand the language. It is often through symbols, pictures, prompting, or through brief hits of knowing in our body. It is in the form of energy, and we just simply miss it. They will use nature, birds, butterflies, and animals to deliver messages by repeating a presence and stressing an action symbolically. This takes some decoding, but with practice, such communication becomes obvious.

At first… we are clueless.

In meditation, while having some internal self-talk, we do not realize the flow of advice coming through. It often blends into the conversation as our own voice. Why isn't this more separate so we can realize them more easily? Because *they* are aspects of *us*. They are not separate, nor are they figments of our imagination. They do not come into our world until we are ready to receive and work with them. Their goal is focused and specific. They serve as spiritual advisers present to aid in our spiritual evolution. Can we evolve without their help? Many "Ascended Masters" have accessed God directly for ascension guidance, but most of us need help.

I realized they show up from all different origins. Ascended Masters, ETs, celestials, angels, archangels, dragons, Native American spirit beings, spirit animals, tree spirits, Avian beings, and those from ancient civilizations such as Lemuria, Atlantis, and ancient Egypt. All show up and have unconditionally devoted themselves to working with me, regardless of my soul origin. This is the spiritual community waiting to work with you. They don't have religion to separate their association with us nor each other. They can be a very diverse group presenting and working together.

We have a *master guide* (our Over Soul or Higher Self) that pulls in other spirits, Ascended Masters, ETs, and those from the angelic realm to assist as necessary. These specialists leave or come and go as needed. We may start with a team, but that may change when we attain a certain level.

I have been asked to join them to be in service in another dimension. We all have Ascended Masters assigned to us, and they change as well. They exclusively present to assist in our ascension, regardless of our awareness of them. With practice, you may experience the presence of beings before you—visually, energetically, or physically. You may hear them clearly. This feels shocking at first because it defies what we know as "real."

We manifest what we are ready to experience. These are manifestations of our self, not separate from who we are. You experience them now because you tuned into that station. They do not leave or go away when you turned the dial. They may have been with you all this time. They are probably with you now, as you read this. They are just at another frequency, just as there are aspects of you existing simultaneously at other dimensions and frequencies.

You are only now learning that we can tune our awareness to other stations and expand the experience of being conscious. There are aspects of you existing at higher dimensions and doing other things than what you are doing right now. I have experienced Ascended Masters who asked me to bilocate to a higher dimension with them to do work in taking down separateness or transmuting suffering. In one instance, Ascended Master Kuthumi asked me to assist in transmuting separateness, which appeared as red wax. It appeared as a massive field strewn across the nation. Overwhelmed, I called over to Kuthumi and asked how to do this, as I am only one person. He said, "Like this…" And in the next moment, I bilocated into a thousand copies of me! It was an incredible experience.

PART V

SOUL AND BEYOND

Chapter 6
SOUL CONNECTION

To connect with anything, we must first quiet ourselves and listen. The same concept applies with our soul. As we learn to live in awareness, the connection to what our soul tells us—our intuition—will strengthen. We will come into the state of knowing more easily and learn to walk in the light of greater purpose. We shift away from ego and, instead, function with the wisdom and knowledge of our past lives, soul family, spirit team, and so on. Through adjusting to higher vibrations and living in awareness, we merge with our soul and develop an awareness of why we are here.

Connection to Our Soul

Your soul is within.

To access your soul, you must raise your frequency to close to that of your soul. It would be reluctant to present at your current frequency, as experiencing such a shift would be too uncomfortable.

To connect, do the "Flow" exercise. Find the subtle energy in the body, make it flow, and practice flowing colors and emotions to get Flow going. Then, ask to flow love. Feel emotional energy flowing. Ask your Higher Self (another name for soul) to raise your frequency by flowing energy into your field. Wait and feel this higher-frequency energy (it feels like tingly sensations around your head and face). If you do not feel it, repeat the request. Bathe in it for a few minutes, then ask for this flowing energy to be stronger. Wait and feel. If it does not feel strong, ask again. Intend to feel this energy strongly.

Before we connect, know that sometimes our soul reneges on connecting due to an imminent lesson it may disrupt. It simply means "Not today." Now, ask your soul to step forward from within you. You will feel a surge of energy emerging, coming forward, moving right through your face and body. You'll feel the energy all around you. Feeling this energy, realize you are standing within your soul, sharing an energy field with it. If the energy feels faint, ask your soul to turn it up—it is holding back to protect you. If you feel nothing, ask again and be patient. If there is still no connection, try again at a different time and practice "Flow" more. Intend this energy expand from the top of your head down to your feet. Once you feel it in your entire body, in every cell, expand it outside of you to the space surrounding you. Bath in this expansive vibrant radiance. Next, try communicating with your soul by asking what I is the most important thing your soul needs you to know right now.

Pull back into your body and wait, letting the answer manifest. There is a channel in your body—from the top of the throat to the sternum—where energy as information seems to flow. You may think you are thinking the answer, but our soul uses our thought process to communicate, so trust what you receive. Just wait there and ask again if you don't hear an answer. Be patient. If you just get one-word answers, ask your soul to elaborate, and press for more specifics. Do not be intimidated. See if you can have a back and forth like a conversation. You can also get a pen and paper and do automatic writing. Write the question and begin to write an answer by first rephrasing the question, then write the answer without pausing—your soul will take over. Keep writing, don't stop, and don't think! Words will come faster than you can write because knowing is faster than thinking. Again, try to respond to your soul with a follow-up question and invite conversation with open ened questions. Be curious!

This takes practice, and the more evidence you see, the more confident you will become. You will be more relaxed, and the more relaxed you are, the more Flow. At times, your soul may not want to answer. The question may have come at a bad time, be too egoic in nature, or be part of a lesson your soul would rather you experience firsthand. At times, it may simply want the question posed differently. If you practice using Flow to connect a few times, you will soon see that you will no longer need to do it. Just intend and ask your soul to step forward. If you practice daily, it becomes conditioned, and you can engage with the presence of your soul throughout the day. Pretty soon, after connecting once in the morning, your soul will be in your presence all day. You must be able to hold frequency for your soul to sustain being present. Keep connecting and strengthening this connection, reconnecting when you can throughout the day. The goal is to connect daily, and after a while, you will not need to, as your unveiled soul will seamlessly blend with you automatically. You will feel it's amazing energy and merge with soul consciousness, developing the experience of knowing rather than thinking. Anchoring soul connection is where you start.

Ask your soul to reveal higher frequency so you are forced to acclimate with upshifts. The goal is to be in this energy all the time. It takes time, but it will happen. Practice communicating with your soul telepathically or through automatic writing or energy.

Practice having regular conversations, so your soul is always a standby adviser eager to steer you in the best direction possible. Get to know each other and share life together. You will be in a higher frequency and become aware of new possibilities.

The energy field of your soul is conscious awareness.

Deepening Conscious Awareness

Conscious awareness is an expanded state of being.

Knowing is experienced via consciousness.

We have a relationship with consciousness because we are in it, and we *are* it. It is the total picture beyond form experience that we so anchor to as reality. It's like being in that rocket ship and not having stars as a reference point. Conscious awareness is being without any reference points. When we are in the energy field of our soul, we do not need reference points. Just *be* without any attachment—attachments are reference points. Just because form appearances exist before me does not mean I need to step down from my view. I can engage with the personality that comes with this spaceship and interact. I do not need a "self" to do this. I do not need an identity to be the greater experience of being. I just feel the expansion and acclimate to that energy. My view is different because I am not self-identified or have any attachments. How I act and what I say may differ, as I am re-experiencing the world through a different lens. It is love-filled, as this expansion is loving energy. I can see where rancid is sourced, but I do not judge. I sense an urgency for that to change to a higher version of what is. I can see the suffering of those creating pain in others and only wish they find healing. I am coming from a loving lens—this is Christ Consciousness. It is Mother Teresa Consciousness. It is Buddha Consciousness. We supercharge our experience of conscious awareness with love.

When we allow ourselves to fill with love, it can be overwhelming. We tear up and flood with compassion. This is not a steady state, but a moment to provide us with a view of intense emotional energy for all that is. It is expansive and blissful. It is self-arising compassion—a moment of deep realization that we are love. It is the complete obliteration of Egoic-I (at least for the moment) and the embrace of all that is. The expansion is infinite.

During a morning meditation, I received this beautiful and profound wisdom from a tree spirit known as "Mago Tree Spirit." Mago and I met at a retreat in upstate New York, at which, Mago became part of a spiritual team, mentoring me through my ascension. Mago had reminded me to practice being heart-centered and to learn to see the soul of all living things. But then went on. "Notice the air around you. This air is a living, breathing consciousness. You are bathing in this consciousness twenty-four seven. Notice as it gently touches your face, as it wraps its arms around you. Expand with it as an expansion of a joined consciousness. This is a path to oneness, as the air connects to all things. You don't need to see this connection, but the air is the connector. Through the air, your combined consciousness is, at once, connected to all consciousnesses. Thus, by changing your vibration, you are changing the vibration of all."

Mago continued to say that practicing this merging with air consciousness would, eventually, create a seamless experience of being as self and spirit at once

Realizing Our Soul

Being one with our soul feels like snuggling up with an old friend and being in love. Our world shifts through this lens as we acclimate and live here. Connect daily, and the connection becomes effortless. A mere intention. The shifts become more dramatic. The energy we feel is visceral, and it is evidence of being real. We can look back on our journey to the present in amazement, knowing what is possible has been lifted. We have learned to trust that in the deep end of the pool, we can let go and float. You can now claim your world through this energy. In consciousness awareness, no limitations or definitions exist.

Try connecting with your soul and launching into meditation.

Remember initially the need to connect anew each day. This threatens our ego, who wants everything solid, static, and permanent.

We eventually will replace ego with our soul and thinking with knowing. Develop a working relationship with your soul by being curious and asking questions. The back and forth will become natural. Enlist your Higher Self as a trustworthy adviser. I noticed that my soul was even planting questions I should ask! Your soul can advise you in every aspect of life. It can advise you on nutrition, medical care, or even what car to buy. Most importantly, my connection to other realms and spiritual beings comes through my soul. All my ascension work happens via my soul and its energy field.

This is experiencing 4D—the fourth dimension. In starting to taste these differences between ego and soul energy, we start to realize ourselves as multidimensional beings. This dual experience is multi-dimensionality. As we open, these other dimensional experiences reveal themselves according to our readiness.

We came here for a reason.

Discovering our Divine Plan connects us partially to why. Each of us, as a soul, has a deeper reason.

Free will is respected, and so it is essential that humans evolve by learning. I am as you—here now to learn. Our purpose is initially defined by lessons, as they prompt us onto a path. Through them, we lift the veil between knowing ourselves as one human incarnate to knowing ourselves beyond this incarnation as we remember past lives and unravel the myths of separateness.

Often, things that happened long ago continue to impact us. We need to move beyond time and its contexts and the limitations of mind. Our soul holds a memory of every incarnation it has experienced. Some of these experiences remain alive and relevant and influence our now, as we also influence the past and possibly the future.

Certain structures ensure we can exist as interdependent beings of energy. Our dimensional structure, a continuum of frequency distribution, resembles the radio dial. Let us imagine being at a time before television when there was only radio. Imagine being a young child listening to this wooden box from which sound is emitted. Now, let's imagine a broken radio that only receives one station. If we were a young child with this broken radio as the only radio we have known, we would believe that there was only one radio station that existed at all. That is where we are at. We experience this 3D frequency radio station. It is all we know, all we ever had access to. Not knowing otherwise means nothing else exists. Now we open ourselves to all stations.

We can be channels of energy. I recall being able to light a light bulb and recharge batteries after a Reiki training. We can experience life at a different frequency, which gives us a different experience of life. We see that within our experience of being, an energy continuum exists. If we go from low to high on the dial, we experience a dramatic shift in our 3D reality. If we raise our frequency high enough, we start to access different stations or channels. This is the edge of the dimensional continuum. People who have elevated their frequency may open to other dimensional experiences that are distinctly different from this 3D experience. In higher dimensions, all is energy, so form is not as we experience. Thought can manifest as energy instantly, and usually lower energy emotional experiences are not able to manifest. We exist simultaneously at multiple levels of energy; thus, we are multi-dimensional capable beings. We can become conscious of such and choose to play or do work on planes parallel to 3D. There are places of healing and transformation in other dimensions, such as stargates, portals, or places of soul origin.

I have been told I am now "omni-dimensional." This reflects the dimensional separations collapsing into the oneness of *knowing*. It's like playing multiple stations on the radio at once. I don't hear them, but I realize them and can access them. I simply filter that experience so I can function in this realm. I access them with intention. You can imagine how confusing it would be if we could hear multiple radio stations at once. Now you can understand why we do not have automatic access to different dimensions. We would not be able to function. Yet important things happen at higher frequencies and being able to access when we choose can help with our individual, as well as collective, evolution. My soul likes to visit stargates, portals, and go home (to Pleiades) when I nap. When I awake, sometimes I can remember fragments of those travels, but most often I don't. I sometimes awaken before I am back in my body, so I must re-enter my body first. I feel as though I just traveled across the universe!

Daily Practice: Connect With Your Soul

Go into meditation and ask your soul to raise your frequency. Bask in this energy bath. Now practice with your eyes open. Notice your chattering mind goes quiet, like in awareness, but also, it pulls back. It shows a more global awareness of not just being, but of what is. Being globally aware has nothing to do with how we self-identify, nothing to do with our story, or even our wonderful accomplishments. We do not separate ourselves from our experience of being, regardless of what that presentation is. We realize the energy of being right now does not attach to or identify in that way. We feel that charge metabolizing energetically. We tune in, but at the same time, we know the news and music are playing elsewhere. We exist multi-dimensionally, and just knowing that expands us.

Knowing who we are, as our soul in origination, helps us refine our multi-dimensionality.

Released Soul Contracts

How do we know when we have learned all our contracted lessons?

We know we have lessons remaining if we still work through challenges and unanswered questions in our life. If you don't experience any rancid-tasting challenges, it is possible you have released your contracted lessons. We may still have non-contracted lessons, but they are not as severe as contracted lessons and are manifested when we are ready to learn from those experiences. Once out of the way, we step into alignment with our Divine Plan—in Divine Flow. It means we do what is suggested, learning to be guided by *knowing*, listening for that soul-directed guidance. Once we engage in that process, Divine Flow gets stronger and becomes clearer to us. We just follow where it directs and watch as our world suddenly gets easier. Our needs and wants merge and manifest before us without effort. When this happens, we work on a path of ascension. We are beyond our contracted lessons. But working beyond our contracted lessons does not mean we can retire, put our feet up, and chill.

There are things a "soul" may want to do or accomplish through the rare opportunity it has as a human incarnate. You are now becoming conscious of what those things are (how exciting!). This is the time to embrace the 4D lens and be aware of your soul's energy field. Additional guidance can be derived from both human and spiritual mentors. Accessing 5D in meditation opens us up to a world of support, meeting and working with your personal spirit team.

Past life lessons have been necessary for me to integrate and work toward my life plan, especially in ascension development. (Note: They are not *my* or *your* past lives, as we are just *one* participant of those lifetimes. They are our *soul's* past lives.) But not everyone must go that route for ascension, as every individual may follow a different path. Once practiced being and relating with Soul, you can ask your Soul to show you what you need to to know from past life experience, and based on readiness your Soul will bring you into that experience. No hypnotherapy required!. After taking time to process that experience, ask again to see if there is another life your Soul wishes you to visit. Spiritual guidance and mentorship speed the process and allow us to learn via knowing. As you go deeper into the ascension process, it becomes a priority over everything else. You will find wonderful support and a sense of nurturing care as you work your way through this soul's plan. There are always more lessons, but they all center around developing into the best version of yourself. You will be directed to books, teachers, classes, and communities. You will make connections that open doors to a whole new beginning. I have found that going within became the ultimate source of what I needed to know.

Your soul is driving, and you finally get to sit back, trust, and enjoy the ride.

I know… being in the back seat and not having any idea of where you are going sounds daunting. But remember, this tests the ego, which demands knowing "where, when, and how." It wants answers immediately. We are used to its impatience because it is more familiar than not *knowing*. Being in the back seat in expectation is like saying, "Give me back those keys!" Notice and gently, without judgment, ask ego to sit back and take a nap. Try to sit back and experiment with *not* knowing, blindly trusting the internal guidance system of your soul.

This is surrender.

We surrender to being.

Realizing the best, highest version of yourself is an act of remembering via *delayering*.

As a soul, everything we need to know and realize is already in place. We go through a delayering process at death as we transition between 3D and the "Astral Plane." We are choosing, in free will, to delayer partially now.

How are these processes different from when we die?

The answer is they overlap. We will end up spending less time delayering if we do it now rather than later in death. The difference lies in energetic shifts that allow 3D densities to fall away. We do not need to shed all our 3D density as we live here. We can simply shed layers that block our soul memory from fully remembering. The information is too overwhelming to know at once, so we need to engage in readying energetically as well as in knowing. The information available to us when we move into a higher plane pertains to an expansion of ideas around realization.

We shift into a greater purpose in helping Earth attain realization—and Earth is also part of a greater intergalactic consciousness that works toward evolution. As per Ma'at, the Egyptian Goddess of

Justice and Balance, Earth will evolve to 5D by 2035, and humanity must evolve too. Therefore, we slowly delayer little bits at a time, as we need to be able to handle these expansive ideas and responsibilities carefully. We begin by releasing what we no longer need, completing our contracted lessons to the best of our awareness. We must become aware of the soul contracts still before us, and we must become aware of new possibilities to pursue a possibility beyond collective understanding.

If we could shed more of the veil and allow who we are beyond our soul to emerge, what would happen? We would experience something like a butterfly emerging from its cocoon. The outer appearance encasing us falls away as the being of light rises—larger and greater than its enclosure. We would expand in form to overtake our physical self.

All may seem the same, aside from not feeling connected, when first we take on this new multidimensional view as a *soul*.

We come to know that all is energy and change.

All can change, and anything is possible. This experience feels immensely powerful because the world is not so solid-feeling as in 3D. We can see the power and influence of energy. Energy can change the world. The energy of love, the vastness of its vibration, has so much healing potential for each of us to realize.

As we acclimate to our new energy, we must physically learn to hold higher frequency. We may need to prepare by hydrating, changing our diet and exercising, or doing yoga. You may feel sick if you are not physically able to hold these energies. Effects can include muscle cramping, hives and rashes, nausea, stomach pain, and headaches. Yoga is an ideal exercise because it balances physical and mental stamina. It mixes the sympathetic and parasympathetic nervous systems into physically stressful postures, teaching us balance and resilience. Daily meditation practice and adequate hydration are essential.

Eventually, we see that it is all energy and malleable. We see there is meaning and purpose.

Meaning in our life is precious. Life without meaning feels empty, so discovering who you are is imperative to understanding *why* you came here. Beyond contracted life lessons, our deeper purpose awaits in our discovery. It is a step into an expansion, realizing our immediate world in which we seek meaning is but one aspect of understanding our higher purpose.

SOUL INCARNATIONS

We are human incarnates of a high-dimensional, energetic being—the soul. Our soul is eternal and has incarnated and lived in places prior to Earth and even prior to Earth's existence. In each place our soul lived, it had incarnated as a being of that civilization. On Earth, our soul incarnated as a human, but on Pleiades, as a Pleiadean. Our soul has had numerous incarnations prior to incarnating as human lives, and each of these lived experiences become our soul's genealogy. So just as if we do Ancestry.com and discover we have some German and Scandinavian DNA, our soul has parts of itself holding these incarnations known as fractals. A fractal is an aspect of each of our souls, based on where and how it incarnated prior to human experiences. Typically, there are three to four main fractals (of possibly many), and they take turns being as you. You can tell the difference because they feel different. You can ask to meet to discuss what they want you to learn from them. Ask to meet each fractal and ask their origin and the order of working with them in ascension. They can be used to implement healing beyond our own capabilities. Soul fractals are of soul origins, including extraterrestrial, angelic or celestial, Ascended Masters, humans, hybrids, or any other type of living organism. The fractals can each provide guidance for ascension and healing. After all fractals complete their ascension, they merge together into one in the experience of oneness.

Our soul may have a large number of prior non-human incarnations, but they exist as parts of our current soul—even though we may have only been exposed to one fractal. We can become conscious of the presence of other fractal experiences. We ask and can formally meet with each part separately. It is our soul's genealogy. We do this with the understanding that these parts are all an integrated aspect of our experience of soul. We experience the fractals as a separate individual experience to learn who they are and the role that fractal has played or will play in our development. You can ask to meet your fractals one at a time and work with them, even spend a day or weeks with them. You will see they have different energies and purposes that may be useful to you.

I once held a townhall-like meeting with my fractals and learned I held Pleiadean, Cassiopean, and Angelic origins. I asked to spend a day with each, and they obliged and shared with me their purpose and the reason why I would switch fractals in the future. We each went on an ascension journey, and then, at a moment of realizing *oneness*, they all merged into one.

Once we experience something like this, we release the idea of fractals being divided and understand that we are not separate from any of these experiences, nor are they separate from each other. Fractals may have a reason to *fractalize*, for specific reasons such as healing others or ascension work. We are the manifested state of fractalization. We are those fractal and whatever presentation (an Ascended being for example) manifests. It could be Christ or an Archangel, it is all a fractalized version of the God realized state of us in oneness. It presents as us channeling these entities but that is separateness- I and that that I am channeling. No separateness, I have fractalized that entity as a manifestation of my God realized state in a form that is required and agreed to in that moment. You may need to get to this level to fully comprehend this experience. Going forward, we may have a hybrid experience where new lessons take place, or one fractal may present exclusively for an extended time to provide what we need. It does not matter, as we are all one with our fractals. We remain in an engaged experience with our deeply multidimensional multifaceted soul, knowing how deep the resources are within.

All our souls were created by God prior to incarnating. In each of us, the oldest fractal will most likely be the connector to Source energy. That fractal will take us on that journey to realizing Source or God. When I first experienced this fractal, I understood it as an ancient part, perhaps older than any earthly thing, relating back to the galactic regressions I had already experienced. Its energy grew rapidly and became overwhelming, though it felt intensely deep and sacred. Words cannot do justice to what I experienced, but I knew it was life-changing. It was pure Source energy—the experience of God, an explosion of all as oneness that extended beyond existence, both known and unknown. I instantly held a knowledge of how we interconnect to the other galaxies and universes. I cannot come close to describing being so expansive, certainly not with any earthly language. This energy was there to be acclimated by human form.

It is divination experienced and provides a gateway to possibilities I could not have imagined, such as other dimensions, parallel experiences, or simultaneous realities. This energy may even have instant healing ability. It exists as a portal of oneness within each of us. You will be redefined by such and understand why we are said to be divine beings in a human form.

Having such a life-changing experience creates explicit and implicit memory of such as a reference point. I could never forget such experiences and will only become more and more familiar with them in the future. I keep expanding and evolving energetically, as there seems to be no limit. In other words, these deep experiences flavor the lens I look through now. They manifest the presence needed to foster growth and expansion. Through them, you can maximize benefit, serving humanity as a service to God. When you reach moments of God-realized energy, you may experience what I call a "wipeout." A wipeout is like having one's hard drive wiped clean.

I recall not being able to access who I was several times—no history, completely unavailable. However, it was temporary, and I had many similar incidents. It buried ego and memory. They followed energy leaps in the ascension process. In the immediate sense, I felt dissociated until the energy calmed down and I managed to acclimate. Once I did, I could function, as I still have different roles to play as a husband, father, therapist-healer, mentor, and even as a student. My Egoic-I has now become extremely difficult to access, and feels like it is off limits, almost walled off.

Chapter 7
PARADIGM OF TRUTH

Everything we have discussed in this book so far has been to point the way to help each reader recognize the divinity within themselves and all around them. None of us exist as separate. Our actions and lives are neither small nor meaningless. We consist of love energy at our very core, from the beginning of creation—only blinded to this by our lack of awareness and ego. This is a truth. Or, at least, one small fraction of what is true.

In this final chapter, we will look at three kinds of truth and their implications.

TRUTH AS A PARADIGM

In divinity, positive and negative experiences have equal value in helping us evolve. This concept is separate from the moral code of right and wrong taught by religious institutions. Truth replaces right and wrong in higher consciousness. We can invite one hundred people into a room to share ideas of right or wrong. We will get one hundred different ideas. Truth has no variable. We explained this earlier as predestined soul contracts complicating our reality and the righteous appearance of meaning. As a human merging with one's soul, *truth* becomes what is distilled of all this.

It is what we came here to learn and realize.

Personal Truths

Truth can be broken down into three areas: personal, collective, and universal.

Personal truth is knowing or realizing eternal truth based on what we need to learn within our personal soul contract. We may, for example, question our worthiness to succeed or be loved. It would take us higher by teaching we were always loveable and worthy and always will be. It is separated from the timelines, so it can be timeless or eternal. Anything we work on in our contract will bring us closer to realizing ourselves as a soul. Thus, this individual work handles realization of truth on a personal level. Our self-manifested reality helps us realize these lessons and they simply repeat, amplified if we fail to learn them. Sometimes our lessons involve or affect others in our life, which brings us to the next truth.

Collective Truths

Collective truths, more global, pertain to large groups of people or beings on the planet.

We have witnessed the horrors of war. War is horrible, and it needs to be, so we hopefully will not choose war. This is a collective truth. We now witness a polarization between political groups, racial and ethnic groups, and gender disparity. All are varying displays of separateness. The idea that we are separate and "our side" is better or superior to yours is a lie. What is not true does not feel good. Acting to sabotage or obstruct the free will of another by mobilizing power over them is fear-based and all sourced in ego. Power and control do not feel good when you are on the receiving end. It does not feel good because it is not a *truth*. The collective truth is that we are all the same and share oneness on a higher level. We are all connected, and when you attack me, you attack yourself. We have been here before, and it is being replayed and amplified because we have failed to realize collective truth.

Is that a good thing or a bad thing?

Is it good that such separateness is amplified in a way to be dysfunctional and intolerable?

No one wants to experience suffering, but suffering has a purpose. It points to our lessons.

Universal Truths

Universal truths revolve around the "bigger picture."

It is from a more pulled back view that we can access such realizations. Earlier in the book, I referenced the George Floyd murder. I used it to illustrate that the event triggered a worldwide movement to bring racial injustice into public scrutiny, unleashing powerful emotions pent up due to the pandemic lockdown. A strange coincidence of timing allowed a young girl to film the entire thing on her phone. That video went viral. I suggested that each of the four policemen, Floyd, and the young girl had overlapping soul contracts agreed to prior to their human incarnations to manifest this event.

This situation served a higher purpose, and the entire world felt the impact, as demonstrated by the worldwide reactions. That is the nature of a universal truth. This is where separation from right and wrong occurs. Floyd had to be unjustly murdered for the good of mankind—that contractual agreement is a truth acted out. It is not that murder is right or wrong. That is not relevant. What is relevant is this needed to happen—as it did, when it did. Look at Earth and notice all the conflicts happening concurrently. Look at how our medical, mental health, and substance abuse communities treat symptoms with toxic pharmacology rather than resolving the underlying issues. Artificial intelligence is emerging and could be an unchecked threat to our planet. Earth has experienced an increase in fires, floods, storms, and earthquakes resulting from manmade climate change. As our beloved home evolves these big lessons, each must become more toxic and painful. Only then will mankind consider yielding to a lesson beyond separateness, power, greed, and selfishness.

I do not want this to happen, but it seems apparently inevitable. Universal truths affect all beings.

The Truths Continuum

Can you accept the paradigm of moral codes and that right or wrong are based on logic and reason?

It's hard because truths are not thought concepts as laws are. Truths are part of an alternate reality. They, in fact, have always been with us as our own reality—only not evident in plain sight. Now, things are amplifying, and if we don't start recognizing what is rancid, our planet will be in deep trouble. We are not too late. When we work on ourselves, shedding the lies embedded in our history, we realize personal truths as to who we are. Can this be moved to a collective experience of realizing truth? Collective truths realized will lead to a universal truth we want to know and realize.

I have laid out this breakdown of truth into three parts so we can more easily learn and understand. But still, they are inseparable and interconnected. We realize our personal truths by interfacing with others working through their own personal truths. The world looks the same as we collectively manifest our surroundings. Our energy shifts to contribute to that more global experience. Our values shift and change and may need to shift even more.

Valuation

The world has its societal and cultural norms. It has a way of defining success and a set of collectively defined and agreed-upon values.

This is called collective valuation.

When we see the world through the lens of truth, our values shift and no longer make sense. For example, should an Emergency Medical Technician (EMT) make a barely livable wage while a talented athlete earns millions to play a game? Is saving lives so much less valued than our entertainment? We may disagree with ideas that our current society or governments sees as virtuous. We may not agree with a valuation system that denies equity or healthcare. ... I could go on and on.

In ancient Lemuria, everyone worked and was valued equally, regardless of what they did—provided they contributed to the collective. I am a licensed Creative Arts Therapist. In New York State, my license is worth less than a social worker only because of politics and lobbying. I am not less in value than my social work peers, and I know my worth. I don't let state laws define how much I can earn or who can access my practice. I overwrite these inequities with my own personal valuation. Many toxic ideas, such as greed and patriarchy, have become embedded and institutionalized within our societal value system. As Earth shifts, we will see an exposure of what needs to be released so truth can be realized.

The realization of truth by our earthly collective will not happen until this exposure-release cycle completes, as it is part of four to five stages of evolution the Earth now undertakes. Our job is to pull back and simply absorb this bigger idea of what happens so we can avoid getting caught up in the unstable feeling. Change of this global nature will be very disruptive to our norm, but we need to let it happen for our ultimate benefit. Do not allow the collective valuation to define us as we evolve and claim a world of higher possibilities.

Our personal valuations are those ideas about us that we actualize as truths: compassion, worthiness, being nonjudgmental, and so on. We do not allow others to define us as we approach the limitlessness of our soul. Definitions limit us, so we stay within our own rules as we decide what we hold as our personal valuation. We know what is important, and we do not let anyone else decide that for us.

Now, let us take this new idea of valuation and truth and see how they connect. Valuation is just one aspect of truth. I must hold fast to my values and ideas in this book, as they challenge collective ideas of possibility and right and wrong.

My strong personal valuation is realized as truth and derived from realized truths. I will not let the collective impart their values on me, and I will not allow anyone to define who I am in truth, as I am beyond such definition. It simply would not be possible.

Personal application of valuation is realizing ourselves in truth, owning this as knowing our inner strength as sovereignty.

Sovereignty

Being sovereign includes realizing that *who you are* and *who you think you are* may be two distinct experiences.

Who we think we are—the ego-identified roles we play out as separate persons—is subject to rules and laws, as well as cultural norms and moral expectations. We honor the concepts and contexts of living on this planet in the third dimension, such as linear time and the concept of right and wrong and accept this patriarchal society. We are subjects of power and control. Wait, you say, I did not sign up for the patriarchal power and control part! No, but it has been collectively manifested, and we must be subject to it to learn from it. I have heard other intuitive people, using their spiritual base as a platform, announcing that we need to reject government-imposed controls attempting to manage the pandemic. This idea stems from ego, as it is fear-based. It teaches that somehow, I will be less sovereign as a soul if I must follow some rules, like wearing a mask, keeping my distance, or taking a vaccine. They could ask me to stand on my head and it would not threaten my sovereignty, as there is no ego to feel threatened. When we are unveiled and integrated as soul, we lift beyond our human incarnation. If we can let ourselves move beyond ego identification and connect with limitlessness and expansion, how can some government mandates in any way define us in measuring our freedom?

Freedom is being so much more than the human we think we are. I am beyond limitation and possibility as I realize all is energy and, thus, all is change. Government threat may serve another function besides keeping us from killing one another. It may amplify the separateness we experience, as groups identify with differences. This feels rancid, as perhaps its higher purpose is to point out we are not separate.

Sovereignty is rising above all this 3D ideation about limits and laws. It is realizing our freedom on a higher plane. It is connecting and understanding that truth will replace right and wrong some day in the future. The fear-based idea that we can be threatened by laws or imposed limitations does not exist. If I break the law and go to jail, my sovereignty is not restricted by the metal bars of my jail cell. I chose to be there, experiencing a consequence of my actions for my learning or to benefit others. I am sovereign prior to my arrest. I am sovereign beyond my arrest. I, as higher frequency, cannot be defined by physical limitation. In one past life regression, I was a slave on an abusive plantation in Georgia. The limitation felt intolerable, but the lesson led me to go within to find freedom. Freedom realized within is not containable by bars or physical limitation. This does not mean living in lawlessness—it is an entirely different paradigm that is only comprehensible at a higher frequency.

We can now define sovereignty as being within our personal valuation, in truth. I, in my freedom, as opposed to being defined by community or societal standards. I claim my sovereignty, in knowing, as inner strength (Divine Masculine), not power. The form appearance resembles power, but that is egoic, and this is soul-based. Think about Samurai. The noble, skilled Samurai does not flaunt his abilities and even keeps his weapons under his robes, arms folded in knowing who he is and his capability as a warrior. He does not have to show, knowing of his inner strength.

As we claim knowing ourselves in truth via the energy of the Divine Masculine, we claim our sovereignty.

Surrender

From my office chair, I look at a person on the blue couch in front of me.

She has courageously brought herself across a difficult threshold—my office doorway. It has taken tremendous effort to get to that couch. She lives in intolerable pain. She is nervous and still, in this moment, wonders internally if she is doing the right thing.

She feels perpetually broken and hopeless. Yet there she is. She has reached a threshold and decided not to tolerate this unproductive and intrusive suffering any longer. She, like those in AA meetings, surrenders.

In Alcoholics Anonymous, they teach that we are powerless to our addiction and must surrender. But an interesting dynamic differentiates this surrender from "helplessness." Surrender means "to yield or give up." But the person before me *chooses* to surrender. Now, in war, if in battle we find ourselves surrounded, we may die if we refuse to give up. The choice is there, but who wants to die? This feels choiceless and is different from the surrender within my client sitting before me. She has *chosen* to surrender, and this, in her case, is truly a choice.

What is she surrendering? Fighting with her pain.

She has decided to take a risk that, despite a lifetime of overwhelming evidence supporting her brokenness, all of it may be a lie. How incredibly amazing is that? How much courage did it take to be there, looking at me with eyes that plead for validation, knowing the words she will say to me will be dead wrong? I notice, and I am conscious of everything she experiences. I see her and empathize with her, but do not (cannot) feel her pain. She, in fact, needs me to be strong enough to witness her—validate her suffering without being hurt by it.

I sit in my chair opposite her, experiencing a consummation of dense crystalline energy that expands my experience of being as one with Christ Consciousness. I cannot feel any suffering of the person before me. I sit in a field of energy that will not allow anything in, and, in fact, flows outward. This moment feels amazing, blazing, and blissful. Back up one-and-a-half-hours prior…

I sit on my couch at home in meditation—a daily ritual before the fifteen-minute drive to my office. During this meditation, I sit and allow my soul to step forward. I feel it moving forward within me, taking over my internal experience. The energy is powerful and dominant. It is comforting for me to experience, but I choose to connect with God, and I surrender. I bathe in this energy and surrender to the experience as it deepens. It gets stronger and stronger, sometimes rapidly. I energetically expand to the size of Earth. Sometimes it becomes so intense that I lose consciousness and will go off in a dream state. That does not last long, and I bring myself back and continue to consciously surrender.

Sometimes information flows in, and other times, I just attempt to anchor my energy before work. There have been moments when the energy was so dense I could not get my flesh to accept it. It took longer to acclimate. My purpose right now is to acclimate to the highest level of energy I can physically hold. I see things in this journey and receive guidance as well. I have learned to trust the process and realize the flow. Learning to surrender at this level, in hindsight, took years and did have moments of conscious surrender, taking courage and discipline. Later, it became less conscious and more automatic. It is healthy to become aware of choosing to surrender as a practice.

Both the client and I sit in a moment of surrender. How different and similar surrender is for us as we obviously engage in different contexts of being. We think of surrender as an end—an end of a journey or battle. However, it is part of a continuum. In surrendering her battle with suffering, my client crosses into a new beginning. One-chapter closes, and a new one is about to be written. Our evolution begins in the present moment, regardless of how much of the past is infused into that experience. We begin here and know we are on the bridge between chapters. Our spiritual ascension is no different as it ebbs and flows, as life ebbs and flows.

Surrender is a catalyst to healing. When we surrender to faith, then healing can occur. When we surrender our ideas of what is possible or not possible, we get out of the way and faith replaces possibility. Faith is unwavering belief. If we have an unwavering belief that the object of healing will heal, we greatly magnify that idea. When that happens, who is doing the healing? The answer is God. God is responsible for all healing regardless of whether you have a conscious belief in God or not. Faithfully flowing energy, knowing this will result in healing, is engaging in faith. Faith is a form of surrender. Now, you let God work through your faith in healing.

Some of you may get to actualize and experience the Living God existing within the highest level of soul consciousness in each of us. It is the most profound experience I have ever known. Knowing this, you can surrender to God when practicing self-healing.

Surrendering to God is our ultimate surrender.

EPILOGUE

Unveiled constantly pushed us to take a step back and see the big picture through the eyes of our soul. The wider angle ideally allows the ideas of causation to be applied so that we can derive meaning from our life experiences. This is not a bad perspective to have in policy writing, for example. Imagine if we set foreign policy from this wider view.

Perhaps we could see better what urgently needs doing when we see the shifts throughout the planet's entirety rather than regionally. Maybe we can pull back and not see a country divided by culture or race or partisanship, but a people who want the same thing: to not suffer. We are drawing lines between red and blue when we all have red and blue blood flowing through us. We are more the same than different. We are all *one* with *all* people in the world. Furthermore, we are one with all that *is*. Pull back more, and we are one with the universe, one with God.

From this elevated view, we can see the Earth is extremely egocentric. Countries perceive themselves as separate or perhaps as the center of their own world. Other regions do the same. The south vs. the north, east vs. west, or if we live "north of the tracks" vs. "south of the tracks."

In isolating ourselves this way, we create a deeper separation.

The people of Earth don't see themselves as members of a planet. We don't have debates about being "Earthlings." That would require a *pulled-back* view. I present a different perspective—a planet of "Soulings."

As a *Souling*, I would not want to be "Earth-centric." Meaning, I would not want to share a view of separateness as a planet inhabitant. I do not think we should view Earth as the center of the universe, even though, for most Earthlings, it is an important unacknowledged value. It embraces planetary separateness. We are not separate, nor are we the center of a vast, ever-changing, and ever-expanding universe. We have an interdependent relationship within our solar system, galaxy, and universe. We are not merely Earthlings; we are occupants of the Milky Way. We are in relationship to other galaxies; we can say we are multigalactic. If we hold the consciousness of being multigalactic, we expand beyond being Earth-centric.

Pulling back has provided a path for us to walk down, leading to healing and transformation. It offers a spiritual lens if we choose to put those glasses on. In writing about these different views, I have been amazed by the process of translating much of what is beyond words into readable language. I have also realized the limitations that language, English in particular, presents. Pulling back seems to open us up to new possibilities and solutions that are not visible up close. It is like having a third party give their point of view, only we are that third party as well.

We are here together as human incarnates for distinct reasons. We did not come here arbitrarily or by accident. We exist to realize *why* we are here. We are to realize the powerful meaning of our life and our story. *Your* story is as meaningful and important as anyone else's, and now you are on a journey to realize that reality and truth.

I have shared that, on my journey, I have been privileged with some stunning information. Accessing it is a privilege, respected, and viewed as sacred. It continues to flow and, no doubt, I will take responsibility to share as necessary as my Divine Plan indicates. I have been given information about being a soul—a Souling. I have also been given information about being *more* than a soul.

Who are we beyond being a soul? Pull back. ..

LETTER FROM THE AUTHOR

You have now engaged in a journey from trauma and even atrocity to hopefully one of love and bliss.

Together we have learned to learn from rancid, to see challenges as lessons, and to understand suffering is experienced by ego. We have learned there are three possible lenses to experience our world through, and we are complicit in the world manifested for us to experience. We have learned tools to help us switch lenses. We have come across new ideas of what is possible or real. We have looked at reality from different views and hopefully tasted energy at different frequencies. We hopefully have transformed by playing with the experiences and tools offered.

If you have a traumatic history, hopefully you are now motivated to do the hard work, knowing what is possible when you have released what is no longer needed. You have learned what the contracted lessons intended. Perhaps I have inspired you to take your own journey, and your path may be different from mine though equally valid. I hold no claim on presenting anything exclusive. Hopefully you have a new ongoing relationship with your soul and will allow your soul to show you a new way to experience our evolving planet.

I hope this is enough to leave you to practice the free will you have. I wish you only unlimited success.

Peace and Love,

Herb

BIBLIOGRAPHY

Alexander, E. III. "Consciousness and the Shifting Scientific Paradigm," Paradigm Explorer Journal of the Scientific and Medical Network, no. 127; (2018): 3-8. https://scientificandmedical.net/project/paradigm-explorer-issue-127m

Alexander, E. Proof of Heaven. Simon and Shuster. NY, 2012. pp. 152-153.

Barry-Jester, Anna M. "How a Big Pharma Company Stalled a Pursuit of Bigger Profits." Propublica.org, October 4, 2023. https://www.propublica.org/article/how-big-pharma-company-stalled-tuberculosis-vaccine-to-pursue-bigger-profits

Brooks, Arthur C. "This Holiday Season, We Can All Learn a Lesson from Beethoven." Washington Post, December 13, 2019. https://www.washingtonpost.com/opinions/this-holiday-season-we-can-all-learn-a-lesson-from-beethoven/2019/12/13/71f21aba-1d0e-11ea-b4c1-fd0d91b60d9e_story.html

Fappler, Maija. "Gretta Thunberg on Being Different is a Superpower." Huffington Post Australia, article archive, September 21, 2019. https://Huffpost.com/archive/au/entry/greta-thunberg-on-having-aspergers-being-different-is-a-superpower_au_5db0644e40cdfe05733161

Hartman, Steve. "A Young Concertgoer Yelled "Wow!" His Grandfather Was More Surprised Than Anyone." CBS News, November 22, 2019. www.cbsnews.com/news/a-young-concertgoer-yelled-wow-his grandfather-was-more-surprised-than-anyone/

Larzarus, Clifford N. "Can Consciousness Exist Outside of the Brain?" Psychology Today, June 26, 2019. https://www.psychologytoday.com/us/blog/think-well/201906/can-consciousness-exist-outside-the-brain

McTaggart, Lynne. The Field. New York: Harper Collins Paperback, 2008.

Whitman, Walt. The Leaves of Grass. Edited by Francis Murphy. Minneapolis: The Franklin Library, 1981.

Williams, Greg. "Patients Recall Death Experiences After Cardiac Arrest." NYU Langone Health, September 14, 2023. https://nyulangone.org/news/patients-recall-death-experience-after-cardiac-arrest

www.ingramcontent.com/pod-product-compliance
Lightning Source LLC
Chambersburg PA
CBHW071703090426
42738CB00009B/1646